STORY CRAFT

STORY CRAFT

REFLECTIONS ON FAITH, CULTURE, AND WRITING

FROM THE AUTHOR OF HANK THE COWDOG

JOHN R. ERICKSON

MAVERICK BOOKS INC.
www.hankthecowdog.com

Patrick Henry College
www.phc.edu

MAVERICK BOOKS
Published by Maverick Books, Inc.
P.O. Box 549, Perryton, TX 79070

10 9 8 7 6 5 4 3 2 1

Library of Congress Control Number: 2009933333

Maverick Books
P.O. Box 549
Perryton, Texas 79070
www.hankthecowdog.com

Patrick Henry College
One Patrick Henry Circle
Purcellville, Virginia 20132
www.phc.edu

Cover Design by Nathan Ellis, nathan@1fj.com

Indexing by Nikki Georgacakis

CONTENTS

Part Two - Faith, Culture, and the Craft of Writing

Part Three - The Top 20: If I Were Teaching a Class on Writing

INTRODUCTION

By Gene Edward Veith, Ph.D.

There is more to the man behind the dog than first meets the eye. John Erickson, who tells his story here, is an author who has sold some 7.5 million books. He is also a cowboy. He is also three credits short of a Master's degree at Harvard University. He is a very funny guy. He is also, as this book will show, a profound cultural critic. He is a businessman, a rancher, and a musician. He is a devoted family man, and he is a Christian who sees his faith reflected in all of life. Though I don't think he realizes it yet, he is also a great teacher.

There is also more to his books about Hank the Cowdog than first meets the eye. Like only the best children's literature, adults can enjoy them just as much as the kids do. Hank may be a dumb dog, but, like other classic literary characters, he takes on a life of his own, so that even his author, I suspect, is curious to see what he will try to do next. The books about Hank's adventures are not just comedies; they are comedies of character, which are the hardest to write but the most satisfying for readers.

The animals, as in the time-honored fables that go back to Aesop, remind us of people, including ourselves. Hank's constant temptation to eat the chickens illuminates our own temptations. Hank's pride is completely counterbalanced by his shortcomings. When we laugh at Hank's blustery ego, we are missing the point if we aren't also laughing at ourselves.

At the same time though, Mr. Erickson's animals are also animals. Hank will take off on an important mission, only to get sidetracked chasing a rabbit, whereupon he forgets what his important mission was. Hank's sidekick Drover, who is also dumb but in a different way, is the kind of tail-wagging, hyper, loyal-but-nervous character that all dog-lovers will recognize. There is not much of an actual mouse in Mickey Mouse, and Bugs Bunny is not very rabbit-like. But with Hank and Drover, despite their talkativeness, you get the essence of dog.

In this book, Mr. Erickson tells us about himself, recounts how he came to write and publish the Hank the Cowdog books, and explains what some of them mean. In a bigger sense, this is a book about vocation. That word, which comes from the Latin word for "calling," refers to the classic Christian teaching that God calls us to different tasks and purposes. We have vocations in the family (as husband or wife; father or mother; son or daughter), in the church (pastor, elder, choir member, Sunday School student), and in our country (elected official, citizen, police officer, soldier).

We also have vocations in the workplace. God gives us skills, gifts, and opportunities that we use to make our living. Not only that, God Himself is in our vocations and works through them. God creates new life by means of fathers and mothers. God gives us our daily bread through the vocation of farmers, bakers, and cooks. God protects us by means of law enforcement officers, firemen, and the military. God gives healing by means of doctors, nurses, and others in the healthcare vocations. God gives us the gifts of technology through scientists, engineers, and factory workers. God creates beauty by means of writers, musicians, and other artists whom He has given the gifts and talents to make works of beauty and meaning.

The purpose of every vocation, according to the old Protestant theologians, is to love and serve our neighbors. Husbands and wives love and serve each other in different ways; parents love and serve their kids, and kids love and serve their parents. The members of a church love and serve each other. A government official is supposed to love and serve the citizens who put him in office, rather than insisting that they serve him. In the workplace, bosses and employees love and serve each other, as they love and serve their customers. A writer is supposed to love and serve his readers. He isn't supposed to corrupt them, or exploit them to make money, or teach them lies. He is supposed to love and serve them by creating works that, to switch to cooking metaphors, are tasty and nutritious.

As has been said, Mr. Erickson is a man with many vocations, and this book tells us about his family, his church, and his community. It tells about his business ventures and his work on his ranch. It focuses, though, on his vocation as a writer. It tells us about the craft of storytelling. It also tells about the interests, the gifts, the opportunities, and even the travails that God used to make him a professional writer.

I would argue that the Hank books themselves are also about vocation. Hank is the Head of Ranch Security. As such, he has responsibilities, duties, and obligations. He also has irresponsibilities, lapses, and failures. In the course of the story, though, he always comes through, rights the wrongs, forgives and is forgiven, and the mutual love and service that everyone on the ranch has to have for each other is restored.

This book is also about integrity. CBS turned Hank the Cowdog into a cartoon episode, but, as Mr. Erickson describes here, the producers literally took the family out of his stories. He refused to let that happen again. Disney wanted to turn the series into an animated movie, but, again, that would mean selling out his characters and his artistic integrity. Many writers, musicians, and other artists are so hungry for commercial success that they compromise their creative integrity—adding sex scenes to movie scripts, toning down religious references in their music, surrendering the creative process to whatever the marketplace wants. But Mr.

Erickson turned down the fame and fortune that Hollywood would bring. Instead, he remained faithful to his artistic vision and to his Christian convictions.

Those convictions mark him as a profoundly Christian artist. But Hank never talks about Jesus, some might object, as if dogs were objects of salvation. Mr. Erickson's vocation is not one of preaching. The Christianity in these stories is not on the surface. It is deeper down. The very structure and the craft of his storytelling: the nature, human nature, and animal nature that he writes about; and the moral truths that even his dogs have to deal with are in accord with the reality that God created. Consequently, as he points out in this book, though his stories do not have a religious content, they have a religious *effect*.

Another dimension of the Christianity in these stories is that they are comedies. That genre does not get the respect of more supposedly "serious" forms, such as tragedy. But it is no accident that some of the greatest Christian writers have always turned to comedy: Dante, Chaucer, Shakespeare (a master of tragedy, too, but his most Christian plays are his comedies), Swift, Chesterton, and in our own day Evelyn Waugh, Flannery O'Connor. This is because Christianity embodies a comic sense of life.

Christians know that we have a happy ending that gives perspective to the absurdities of life. The Greek and Roman pagans, by contrast, had a tragic sense of life, believing that everyone eventually ends up in Hades, meaning that the few moments we have on earth constitute the only happiness we are likely to get, and when those don't turn out so well, it is tragic. Both comedy and tragedy deal with pride. Tragedy fills us with pity and fear at the way the inflated ego gets knocked down to size. Comedy, on the other hand, shows us the inflated ego and makes us see how ridiculous it is, making us laugh. Tragedy and comedy, crying and laughter, both have their place, but comedy is an artform that is particularly congenial to a faith that recognizes just how limited and sinful we all are, but that God has redeemed us anyway and resolves our lives with a happy ending.

Another one of Mr. Erickson's vocations is as a teacher. This is a calling he has taken on more recently. Last summer, he invited onto his ranch ten of our students here at Patrick Henry College for a week of learning about writing. Mr. Erickson taught them about writing not only by giving them pointers of his craft. Since writing has to emerge from the author's life experiences, he gave the students life experiences, such as having them brand cattle. Helping with chores on the ranch, hiking through the canyon, fixing meals, singing songs, and being mentored not only by Mr. Erickson but also by his wife Kris—all the while writing and talking about writing—turned out to be, so the students tell me, one of the highlights of their education.

Along that line, the last section of this book gives advice to young writers. Mr. Erickson teaches writing as a craft, which is the classical approach, not in the modern vein as a vehicle for romantic self-indulgence. (In Mr. Erickson's words, "arrogance, irresponsibility, vulgarity, disrespect, and wild, suicidal self-indulgence.") Mr. Erickson shows a better way, one that can teach Christians how to be the writers, artists, and culture-makers that gave us Western civilization.

This book focuses on the vocation of the writer. But it also works as a guide for anyone trying to find and live out his or her vocations, whatever they may be. The lessons of this book—perseverance, integrity, goodness, God's design—apply not just to writing but to every kind of calling, from running a business, to having a family, or to being the Head of Ranch Security.

FOREWORD

By Nancy Pearcey, Ph.D.
Author of *Total Truth: Liberating Christianity from Its Cultural Captivity*

John Erickson has been spreading his magic in our home for years. The first time I met his famous character Hank the Cowdog, I was in the library hunting for books on tape for my son Michael, who is an auditory learner. My eye was caught by the cover of *Murder in the Middle Pasture,* which features a tough-looking dog surrounded by snarling coyotes, an image that hinted alluringly of danger and adventure. But I thought (mistakenly, as it turned out) that the book was a murder mystery, which Michael did not care for. I walked away, then came back—three times— before picking it up and placing it in my basket.

The next step was getting Michael interested in the story. I simply slipped the first cassette into a tape deck and started listening myself. Soon I was chuckling, then laughing. "What? What's funny? Play it again." Nothing snares a child's interest more quickly than sensing that there's a joke, and he's not getting it.

Over the next four years, Michael listened to every tape in the series—most of them several times over. The action is centered on a family ranch owned by High Loper and his wife Sally May, with their son Little Alfred. Helping out is a ranch hand named Slim Chance. But the real heroes are the animals: the brash but loveable Hank, his skittish sidekick Drover, an intellectual bird dog named Plato, a fast-talking raccoon, a couple of backwoods buzzards, and a clan of uncouth coyotes. They grew to be Michael's near-daily companions. Their silly antics got him through the drudgery of doing chores. Their voices welcomed him home like friends after a busy day. Their familiar episodes often soothed him to sleep at night. As parents, Rick and I were happy to note that listening to Hank stories increased Michael's vocabulary, encouraged linear thinking, and enhanced his attention span. Most of all, though, the stories were plain good fun.

When an author's stories have such a deep impact on our lives, we are keen to learn more about him— what he is like in ordinary life, what he enjoys doing, and how he got to be the writer he is today. Those are the questions John Erickson addresses in this very human and engaging book. He opens his life and heart to readers. We learn about his search as a young man for his own authorial voice, toiling through graduate studies at Harvard Divinity School. We share his amused surprise when his best character turns out to be a cowdog with a corny sense of humor. Erickson then takes us along during the risky, hard-scrabble years of starting up a company to self-publish the Hank books, selling them out of the back of a pick-up truck at rodeos and county fairs. He recounts his struggles to protect the integrity of the Hank stories against the forces of Big Media eager to exploit his creative work for commercial gain. Finally, he answers the frequent queries sent in by aspiring writers asking for tips and advice. He opens his study door and invites us to sit for a spell and watch him at work.

The portrait that emerges is of a cowboy who is personable, funny, down-to-earth, and neighborly, governed by a firm commitment to treating people right. In fact, just the kind of person whose authorial vision one detects through the Hank books themselves. The plot lines may be hilariously convoluted, but they always assume a stable moral universe that can be counted on when characters have to make tough decisions—even when those decisions involve canine concerns like whether to eat Sally May's chickens or nab Slim's cookies. Hank may be comically self-important, constantly inflating his job as Head of Ranch Security. But in the end he always comes through and does the right thing, whether it's saving little girls from a killer horse or rescuing High Loper from quicksand.

C. S. Lewis once said that the books with the greatest impact on the world are not the ones where the Christian perspective is explicit but where it is implicit, woven in and through the subject matter. In his words, "What we want is not more little books about Christianity, but more little books by Christians on other subjects—with their Christianity latent." In fiction, this means stories that do not quote biblical texts so much as show readers what the world looks like through the realism of a biblical lens. Stories that express a biblical worldview through their portrayal of character, conflict, and resolution. In the Hank series, the sense of moral order is clearly derived from Christianity (the human characters treat church as a natural part of life), but it is woven into the background fabric of the stories. Universal themes, like being responsible and fulfilling one's obligations, emerge through accounts of daily life on a west Texas ranch.

Of course, that is the way moral universals are always embodied. Each of us is called to live out eternal truths within the contingent situation in which we find ourselves. That's why regional stories like Hank have such evocative power. When we read descriptions of local customs and settings, we sense a parallel to the particularity of our own lives. It's why we all laugh at Garrison Keillor's jokes, even if we are not Scandinavian. And why *My Big Fat Greek Wedding* was a hit movie, even among viewers who are not Greek. And why *Gone with the Wind* is one of the all-time most popular novels, even among readers who are not Southern. The most revered American writer, Mark Twain, constructed his stories from the raw materials of life in his boyhood home of Hannibal, Missouri, in the nineteenth century. Yet today every schoolchild reads *Tom Sawyer* and *Huck Finn*. The best writers weave universal human themes into the idiosyncrasies of characters and cultures rooted in a particular time and place.

Many readers will enjoy the Hank stories without ever recognizing their deep roots within a biblical worldview, just as fans of Lewis's Narnia series may be unaware of its Christian symbolism. Yet as Western society grows more secularized, even what Lewis called "latent" Christianity tends to stand out more sharply. More than once, as John Erickson relates in these pages, a secularized media has tried to challenge and change the core worldview in his Hank books.

For example, several years ago CBS decided to include a Hank story in a special cartoon series for kids—a real honor for an up-and-coming author. When the episode appeared, however, John was astonished to discover that the story was no longer set on a family ranch. Oh, High Loper and Sally May were still there. But they were no longer married. Instead Sally May had been promoted to ranch boss, while Loper was demoted to ranch hand, alongside Slim. Their son, Little Alfred, had disappeared altogether. The three adults lived together in a kind of bunkhouse. What had happened to the family at the heart of the story?

It turned out that Hank had been subverted by the forces of political correctness. The screenwriters apparently regarded family as an outmoded social institution, and marriage as a means of oppressing women. And so, without bothering to ask permission from the author, CBS had converted his humorous animal tale into a platform for a politically correct ideology. Even the most fundamental moral concepts, such as a positive view of marriage and family, can be "too Christian" to pass muster in today's secularized media.

To stand up to that sort of intellectual imperialism takes courage and determination. And John Erickson is nothing if not determined. He is a self-starter who has learned to circumvent both secular Big Media and ghettoized Christian publishing to get his books into the hands of readers who love them. The reason he writes so effectively is that he insists on writing from what he has lived.

I met John in person for the first time while visiting my parents in Lubbock, Texas. On arriving, I praised the Hank books to my mother (who has a Ph.D. in education) and to our amazement, the newspaper announced that John was slated to present a program at the local library the very next day. It was easy to pick him out of the crowd: He was the one wearing a ten-gallon hat, fringed Western shirt, and cowboy boots. I waited while a long line of people snaked past the book signing table, then shook John's hand and explained that I could not buy any books since there was no room in our suitcases . . . because we had brought four sets of Hank books and tapes with us from home!

Our family will always be grateful for the way John Erickson's books have shaped our lives. Turn the page and enjoy his account of how he became a master story-teller. And if you've ever considered saddling up as a writer yourself, this is a good place to begin to learn the art of storycraft.

AUTHOR'S NOTE

The plan of this book is straightforward. Part One is mostly a personal memoir that describes my apprentice years and how I found my life's vocation with Hank. Part Two deals with writing theory as it relates to culture and faith, and, in Part Three, I offer how-to advice to aspiring writers.

The system I use in documenting my research follows this pattern: [Lewis 2001:49]. It is a system used by archeologists, and I have found it to be the least cumbersome of the several methods of footnoting. It gives us the name of the author, the publication date of the source, and the page number. Most readers won't do anything with that information, but those who wish to trace the source can find it listed in the bibliography.

I would like to thank the people who read this book in manuscript and made suggestions on how to improve it: George Clay, Gene Edward Veith, Nancy Pearcey, Nathan Johnson, Nathan Dahlstrom, Chuck Milner, Mark Erickson, Sandra Morrow, Nikki Georgacakis, Gary Rinker, Ann Rinker, Janee McCartor, and Kris Erickson.

I owe a special debt of gratitude to Nancy Pearcey and Gene Edward Veith, who encouraged me to publish the book, and were kind enough to write introductory essays for it when they had plenty of other demands on their time. Their books on faith and culture have played an enormous role in helping me understand my job as a producer of cultural material in the present age. I have been blessed by their writing and by their friendship.

I am also grateful to my editor, Richard Pearcey, for sound professional advice; to Nikki Georgacakis, a student at Patrick Henry College, who served as my assistant in the summer of 2009, and guided this book through the publishing process; and to Tim and Lyndsay Lambert of the Texas Home School Coalition, whose magazine, *The THSC Review*, published some of this material in article form.

And, of course, my most profound thanks must go to my wife Kris. For forty-two years she has been a friend, companion, help-mate, teacher, and source of wisdom and inspiration. "Her price is far above rubies. The heart of her husband doth safely trust her, so that he shall have no need of spoil . . . She is like the merchants' ships; she bringeth food from afar." (Proverbs 31:10-14)

JRE
JULY 2009
M-CROSS RANCH
ROBERTS COUNTY, TEXAS

- PART ONE -

ONE WRITER'S JOURNEY

- Chapter One -

Not An Ordinary Job

"(Christians) should be known as people in love with the beauties of nature and the wonders of human creativity."
                                                          - Nancy Pearcey, *Total Truth*

In 1982, I started Maverick Books in my garage and self-published the first Hank the Cowdog story. Much to my surprise, it sold well, and everywhere I went, people were telling me, "You need to do more with that dog."

Doing more with "that dog" wasn't something that had ever occurred to me. I thought it was a nice little story, full of earthy humor, but as far as it being "good" in any kind of literary sense . . . how good can a book be, if it's narrated by a ranch dog in Texas?

I gave a copy to a friend who had been living abroad for several years. He was well-read, educated in philosophy and literature, and knew that I had aspirations of being a man of letters in the grand tradition of Melville, Twain, Dickens, Hemingway, and Faulkner.

A few days later, I saw him again. He had read my book. With an odd twinkle in his eyes, he said, "What would you think if you were remembered as the author of Hank the Cowdog?" I glared at him for a moment and growled, "I wouldn't like it at all!" He had seen something special in the Hank story. I had not.

Today, twenty-seven years and fifty-four Hank books later, my dream of becoming a famous novelist has faded away, replaced by something I never anticipated: a vocation as a crafter of stories about a dog. Where I have ended up is not where I thought I was going; it's much better.

I feel like a frog that has been swept over Niagara Falls and finds himself drifting along in a wide placid river. I hear the roar of the falls in the background and see flecks of foam floating past, and I'm struck with wonder that things have turned out so well.

In the beginning, Hank worked for me. Now I work for the dog, and it has been a wonderful adventure. My stories have found their way into homes and schools and churches; deer blinds and hunting camps; hospital rooms and libraries; also in the military barracks of Iraq and Afghanistan; isolated cowboy shacks and missionary schools; into bedrooms where children are preparing for sleep and into homes where a loved one has died.

Somehow I've managed to find the right audience—or they found me—and the Hank books and audios have sold more than seven and a half million copies. Most authors would find that number respectable, and maybe it qualifies me to write the present volume, which we might describe as a series of meditations on the craft of writing.

Anyone who writes "meditations" and talks about his "vocation" has probably been snooping around in theology, and I admit to doing some of that. Gene Edward Veith tells us, "The doctrine of vocation—explored most deeply in the writers of the Reformation, especially Martin Luther—teaches how God calls human beings into different relationships, roles, and realms of service." [Veith 2008:152]

I didn't start my writing career with any notion that it would acquire religious overtones, but it has turned out that way. When parents and teachers allow you to touch the souls of their children, after a while you realize that you're not involved in a purely secular enterprise.

When I started working on this project, I thought it would be a series of how-to essays about the craft of writing, aimed at a small audience of teachers and aspiring authors. But the more I wrote and thought about the subject, the more I wanted to talk about writing in a context of faith and culture, speaking to readers as dignified human beings, whether Christian or not.

As a young writer, I gave more thought to culture than to faith, but with experience and time, I've come to see faith as the incubator of culture, with a well-grounded worldview crucial to solid work.

Francis Schaeffer asked, "How can art be sufficiently meaningful? If it is offered up merely before men, then it does not have a sufficient integration point." [Schaeffer 1973:37] If art and writing have no connection to a transcendent source of law and morality, they are likely to serve no higher purpose than to amuse the artist, and perhaps help a successful writer pay the bills.

For several years now I've come to view my writing in a Christian context, but this is the first time I've written a book about it. The voice of prudence tells me that I should stick with what I do best (humor) and leave the heavier stuff to scholars who are better qualified: Gene Edward Veith, Nancy Pearcey, Marvin Olasky, C.S. Lewis, and Francis Schaeffer, to mention a few who have guided my steps.

But I am alarmed by the slide of American popular culture toward things that are coarse, ugly, violent, self-directed, obscene, profane, visual, and non-rational, and by a parallel development that we might call the

"Santa-Clausation" of culture—the detachment of an event (the birth of Christ) or a creative endeavor (books, movies, music) from the spiritual and historical sources that give them meaning. It is no accident, I think, that we find these two developments side-by-side at this point in history.

A good deal of popular culture is offensive to me. Some of it strikes me as poisonous, and since I'm in the business of producing cultural material and have spent quite a bit of time trying to protect it, another voice in my head whispers that maybe I should talk about this. As a writer, I am convinced by the evidence that a purely secular worldview will poison art at its roots, and without roots it won't survive. "Art that attacks all standards ends up destroying itself." [Pearcey, Fickett, and Colson 1999:447]

The Apostle Paul gives writers and artists a brief but comprehensive mandate that can guide us in our creative work: "Finally, brothers, whatever is true, whatever is noble, whatever is right, whatever is pure, whatever is lovely, whatever is admirable—if anything is excellent or praiseworthy—think about such things . . . and put [them] into practice" (Philippians 4:8 NIV).

Paul is not just telling us how to behave in church. He's giving us a set of ethical criteria that can be applied to aesthetics and incorporated into our creative endeavors. The same qualities that can guide us toward proper choices in daily living can also help us make humane and healthy choices in producing books, movies, sculpture, paintings, and music that are aesthetically good, pleasing, and nourishing to the human spirit—cultural artifacts that offer an alternative to what C.S. Lewis called "the long and terrible story of man trying to find something other than God which will make him happy." [Lewis 2001:49]

Because our age is ugly in many ways, now and then I have to

4

remind myself that we live in a golden moment of time, free from most of the miseries that stalked my great-grandparents on the West Texas frontier in the 1880s: rotten teeth, chronic sinus infections, poor nutrition, isolation and darkness, heat and cold, endless labor, and babies who died in a parent's arms.

There was ugliness in those times too. And, come to think of it, the ages of Paul, Jesus, and Moses weren't so great either. Ramses II slaughtered male babies, and the lofty Roman Empire crucified prophets. I'm glad to be alive at this time in history. If that doesn't always come through in these pages, it should.

CHAPTER TWO

"JUST A MOTHER"

*"Train up a child in the way he should go: and when he is old,
he will not depart from it."* - Proverbs 22:6

When I was growing up, nobody from my hometown had ever become a writer, had even thought about it, as far as I know. The people in my family and community had struggled through the Great Depression, the disastrous droughts of the Thirties and Fifties, and World War II, and that had left them little time to think about writing anything longer than an occasional letter.

Our cultural materials came from New York City, Los Angeles, and London, and it never occurred to us that a kid from Perryton, Texas, could be a part of that enterprise.

I did very little writing until my senior year in high school, when Annie Love, my English teacher, forced us to write an original poem. Most of my comrades on the football team groaned and complained. I wrote the poem and found that it was easy, and spent the rest of the semester writing poems for Mrs. Love. That was first time I realized that I might have a gift for writing.

At the University of Texas, I took some classes on writing and did well in courses that required essays. In my second year at Harvard Divinity School, I enrolled in a year-long class on fiction writing. But I've come to realize that the best instruction I received on writing didn't occur in a classroom or come from someone with a doctorate in English literature.

It came from a woman who never went to college, had never written anything longer than a letter, and had no credentials that said she was qualified to teach. She was "just a mother." My mother, Anna Beth Curry Erickson.

She was a rancher's daughter from the prairie country around Lubbock, descended from sturdy pioneers who had received little formal education but had acquired a reverence for the written word. They were People of the Book and their book was the King James Bible. They knew it well and their everyday conversations were shaped by its wisdom and cadences. At an early age, the KJV was written on my soul.

When I was five, Mother kept me at home instead of sending me to kindergarten. That year, we homeschooled, though neither of us had ever heard that term before. During the day, I followed her around the house and yard as she did her chores: cooking, washing dishes, canning vegetables, hanging out laundry on the clothes line, making beds, and tending the garden.

While she worked, she told me stories about the cowboys, ranchers, and strong pioneer women in our family. She was a wonderful storyteller with a gentle, earthy sense of humor, and those stories and characters ignited my imagination. (I give a full account of Mother's family in my book *Prairie Gothic*).

In the afternoon, she read aloud to me, mostly *Hurlbut's Stories From the Bible.* At the age of five, my heroes were David, Samuel, Joseph, Samson, and Moses. And more than once, she closed the book and said, "John, God has given you a talent too. You must guard it and use it wisely."

Maybe that's something every mother says to every child, but I believed her. She didn't know that my talent would lead me into a career as a professional writer, and didn't live long enough to read my first book. Yet through some miracle of motherly instinct, she gave me exactly the five elements I needed thirty-five years later when I wrote the first Hank the Cowdog story:

1. Respect for the written word.
2. Simple storytelling about admirable characters.
3. Gentle humor, without anger, malice, or ridicule.
4. Worthy role models: Moses and David instead of athletes or "stars."
5. A sense that I should use my talent for something larger than myself.

As parents, we don't always know if our kids are listening to the things we tell them, but I was listening. Decades later, when I was grown and trying to figure out how to be an author, and getting hundreds of rejection slips from publishing houses, I still believed that God had given me a talent and that I should use it wisely.

If I hadn't believed in something larger than myself, I would have given up. What kept me going in those dark times was nothing I had learned in a college classroom, but rather those two simple sentences spoken by my mother: "John, God has given you a talent too. You must guard it and use it wisely."

How do we measure the importance of a mother? For me, it's millions of Hank the Cowdog books and the innocent laughter of the families who read them. When I hear a woman say, "I'm just a mother," I have to smile.

My "just a mother" was the most important teacher I ever had. She's the one who instilled in me a sense of vocation.

CHAPTER THREE

HANK THE COWDOG: A BRIEF HISTORY

"Some of God's greatest gifts are unanswered prayers."
- Garth Brooks, quoting a wise mother from long ago

As a young man, I knew that being a writer was something special, but I didn't want any part of it. Unless you went to work for a newspaper or a magazine, which I never cared to do, your chances of making a living were very small.

I considered several other professions: law, politics, psychology, teaching, ministry. None of those seemed to fit. For me, the moment of truth arrived in 1967 when I married Kristine Dykema, a beautiful dark-eyed young lady from Dallas. We married in August and drove to Cambridge, Massachusetts, where I began my second year as a student at Harvard Divinity School (HDS).

I went to divinity school to find out if the ministry was right for me, and chose Harvard because I needed to know if a kid from a little town in Texas could compete in such a place. I didn't have the grades or SAT scores to get into a top-tier university, but somehow I made it through the admissions process, probably on the strength of the essays they required on the admissions form. By the age of twenty-two, I could write a solid essay.

Harvard was an exciting place to spend two years. Strolling across the campus, I caught glimpses of John Kenneth Galbraith (noted economist and author), Edwin O. Rieshauer (former ambassador to Japan), John K. Fairbank (expert on China), and B.F. Skinner (acclaimed rat-running psychologist whose ideas I detested). Once I sat in on a class taught by a man whose name would soon become familiar, Henry Kissinger.

At the divinity school, I took courses under Krister Stendhal, Herbert Richardson, H. Richard Niebuhr, Harvey Cox, and Gordon Kauffman. Their intelligence and fluency in theology filled in some gaps in the knowledge I'd received at the University of Texas, where a "broad liberal arts education" included hardly a mention of the most influential book in all of Western civilization, the Bible. Or maybe they mentioned it and I just wasn't listening.

Looking back, I regret that I didn't take any courses in Old Testament, because the faculty at HDS had some of the best Middle Eastern scholars in the world. G. Ernest Wright was an expert on Old Testament archeology. Frank Moore Cross and John Strugnell played a major role in translating and interpreting the Dead Sea Scrolls.

Forty years later, I developed an interest in biblical archeology and found myself reading books and articles by Wright, Cross, and Strugnell. Forty years later. Ah, the follies of youth.

I took a course taught by David Riesman, a scholar of national reputation, and talked to him several times in his office. He was a delightful man, kind and down to earth. My term paper in that class was an essay on the religious views of Norman Thomas, who, as a young man, had studied for the Presbyterian ministry at Union Theological Seminary.

Dr. Riesman arranged for me to go down to New York and interview Mr. Thomas, and we met at his office in Manhattan. He was ninety years old, snow-haired, and almost blind, but still tall, dignified, and handsome in his three-piece suit.

Dr. Riesman liked my paper and gave me an A-plus, the only such mark I managed to snare in two years at Harvard. Typically, it came from my ability to write.

In my second year, I took Professor Theodore Morrison's two-semester course on fiction writing, and listened to my fellow students read their stories aloud in the same sedate, paneled room where John Updike and Norman Mailer had once sat as undergraduates. I can't say that I learned much in the class, but it did give me a reason to start writing every day, one or two hours in the morning.

Writers *write,* and professional writers must develop the habit of writing in a disciplined manner. And so it was that, without fanfare, I made the decision to behave as though I were actually a writer.

Much of my motivation came from the fact that I had married a woman with high standards. I knew that Kris would never be proud if I continued on my course of being a careless lout. Her mere presence in my life forced me to reach beyond myself, and in the process of trying to conceal from her what I actually was, I became what I should have been.

I started thinking of myself as a novelist—a *serious* novelist, if you please, one who would write important novels about important subjects and important places. At that point, if someone had told me, "By the year 1985 you will be best known for a series of humorous books narrated by a ranch dog in Texas," I would have laughed.

Me, write humorous books about a dog? No way!

I spent my second year at Harvard trying to write novels that were serious and literary and important. Unfortunately, they were also dull and depressing. Only later did I realize that I was imitating a literary fashion

11

that had an appetite for darkness.

By the end of the 1968 school year, I knew that I was not cut out for the parish ministry or a church-related career. Kris and I packed our few possessions into a small U-Haul trailer and headed back to Texas. An overnight stop in Chicago lightened our load. Someone broke into our trailer and stole most of our worldly goods, including a number of wedding gifts and my five-string banjo. Apparently, everyone but me knew that you should never park a loaded trailer overnight in downtown Chicago.

I left Harvard Divinity School only three hours short of a master's degree in theology and thought I would go back and finish the degree, but never did. I began to realize that anything I could do with a master's degree, I shouldn't do. I had already decided against the ministry, and that left only teaching. I knew that I would enjoy teaching, and that I had the equipment to be a good teacher, but I also felt that teaching would tap into the same energy source that was driving me to write.

It wasn't possible for me to do both, and when I decided not to take the master's degree, I burned a bridge that might have allowed me to escape the hardships that lay ahead. I've never regretted that decision.

Kris and I returned to Texas and lived for two years in Austin. Then in 1970 we paid a visit to my parents in Perryton . . . and somehow we never got around to leaving. I took a job as a farm hand which, after six years of higher education, was the only practical skill I possessed.

Between 1971 and 1973 I had the unusual experience of tending bar in a county that had voted itself legally "dry." Texans have proved themselves very clever at slipping around their own liquor laws, and the country club where I worked was one of five bars that did a brisk business in our "dry" county. I hated almost every minute of my three years of tending bar (see Chapter Eighteen for more details), but it was a job that allowed me to write every morning for three or four hours.

In 1974 I was offered a job managing a 5,000-acre cattle ranch in the Oklahoma Panhandle. Although I still didn't consider ranch life a worthy subject for a writer, I had a feeling that it was a door I was supposed to enter.

That was the beginning of a long apprenticeship that lasted until 1982. I spent most of those years working as a cowboy on three different ranches. I must have inherited some cowboy genes from my mother's side of the family. I loved the isolation, danger, and adventure of the horseback life, and I was good at it. Years later, the University of North Texas Press published seven of my nonfiction books on the subject, but they have lived in the shadow of Hank the Cowdog, and few people even know they exist.

Ranch work provided me with a good foundation for my writing. I acquired a body of experiences that gave me stories to tell and characters that were worth writing about. I also had plenty of time to think about two questions that vexed me: What is a story and what should it do? Those were simple questions, but they didn't have simple answers. I deal with this subject in more detail in Chapter Ten.

Another benefit that came from my cowboy years was that I found the writing voice that was most comfortable for me. I suppose that every young writer goes through a period of experimenting with different voices. It's a bit like spending time in a store full of costumes and disguises. You try on your Hemingway disguise, then Tolstoy, then Dickens and Twain and Faulkner and Joyce, Mailer, Vidal, Margaret Mitchell, Elmer Kelton, Dumas. The list is endless.

In my case, all of this experimental writing went to the trash, so future generations will be spared the embarrassment of seeing me running wild through the costume store.

After years of trial and error, I finally began imitating the oral tradition of storytelling used by cowboys and ranch people in the Panhandle. It was the simple, unadorned approach to language my mother had used in her storytelling, language that crackled with sly wit, subtlety, and imaginative ways of putting words together.

I liked the way country people told stories, and after wearing this costume for a while, I discovered that I was no longer trying on clothes. The costume had become my skin. It was me, and I found an outlet for my stories in livestock publications: *Livestock Weekly, The Cattleman,* and *Western Horseman.*

All of this apprentice work came together in the winter of 1981. I was working as a cowboy on the LZ Ranch south of Perryton, and rising early (4:30 or 5:00 a.m.) to do my writing. I began working on a series of short humorous pieces for *The Cattleman* magazine, about my experiences in the cowboy trade. I needed twelve of them and wrote them as fast as I could. It never occurred to me that they might be good. My only thought was that we needed money to pay for baby clothes and doctor bills.

After turning out six or seven pieces about my cowboy work, I ran out of ideas and thought that it might be fun to write a story from the point of view of a ranch dog. I wasn't sure I could get by with this, because *The Cattleman* didn't publish fiction. Nevertheless, I took a run at it and chose a dog named Hank as the narrator.

I had known an Australian shepherd dog named Hank who lived on a ranch in Oklahoma, and he had been typical of most of the dogs I had grown up with: sincere, good hearted, and by human reckoning, not very smart. Poor old Hank was always in trouble but never understood why.

Drover, another character in the first story, was a little mutt I had known on a ranch in Texas, and I described him just as he had appeared to me: dreamy, innocent, and afraid of almost everything.

To this mix, I added a cat named Pete, a cowboy named Slim Chance, and the man and wife who owned the ranch, Loper and Sally May. At the time I wrote the first Hank story, the character who most resembled me was Slim, the bachelor cowboy, and in many ways he still does. He reads every issue of *Livestock Weekly* from cover to cover, sings to his dogs, eats boiled turkey necks, and puts his dirty dishes into the deep freeze so they won't get moldy. He's my kind of feller.

When I wrote that first Hank story, called "Confessions of a Cow-dog" (it later appeared in a book called *The Devil in Texas and Other Cowboy Tales*), I didn't think it was anything special. I never dreamed there was magic in those characters or that, a few years later, I would end up working for the dog. Paul Horn, editor of *The Cattleman*, never said a word about it being fiction, and may he enjoy a thousand blessings for that.

Several years later, after I had self-published four or five of the Hank books, *The Cattleman* began running the books as serial stories. They ran a Hank chapter in every monthly issue for seventeen years, and it became one of the most popular features of the magazine, a magazine that "didn't publish fiction."

In my travels over the years, I have met many a rancher's wife who whispered, "My husband used to sit at the mailbox in his pickup, waiting for *The Cattleman* to come so he could find out what happened to old

Hank." Those crusty ranchers were too cheap to buy a book, but they sure enjoyed Hank's adventures in the magazine.

My writing for livestock publications gave me the freedom to develop a set of rural characters who spoke for themselves and viewed the world in their own terms, without political correctness or the intrusion of urban minded mediators who, secretly or not so secretly, believed that rural meant "dumb." That is a common error made by people who have never spent any time in rural America and who often describe us as "provincial."

We're not provincial. *They* are. We read their magazines, attend their movies, and listen to their news broadcasts. We know a lot about them. They know nothing about us.

By the year 1982, I had served a long apprenticeship as a writer. I hadn't cheated or taken short cuts. I had been writing four and a half hours every day, seven days a week, for fifteen years. I had collected at least one thousand rejection slips and was ready for someone in the publishing community to give me a chance to practice my craft. When that opportunity didn't come, I started my own publishing company in my garage. That's a long story and I'll deal with it in the next chapter.

If I had waited for the approval of Eastern publishers, I doubt that Hank the Cowdog would have ever seen the light of day. The stories were too "country," too "regional," too quirky and eccentric, and they didn't fit into any of the accepted categories of popular fiction. *What were they*? Were they westerns, detective stories, pet stories, humor, adventure, Texana, or children's literature?

Those are questions that editors and store managers ask. I really didn't care. All I knew was that people were buying them.

16

With no one to answer to except my banker and my customers, I wrote books that were fun and full of play and gentle humor. In the spring of 1983, we brought out the first Hank the Cowdog book, and also a cassette tape version, with me doing the voices of all the characters. We followed it six months later with the second Hank title. These books were a hit from the beginning (in a very small, rural setting), and it was then that I began to think of making the Hank books into a series.

Back in those days, we were selling through the mail and at my speaking appearances, and the original audience for the Hank stories was 100% adult, mostly people involved in agriculture. I had never intended the stories to be for children, and it's a good thing I didn't. If I had set out to write children's stories, I would have assumed that children were not capable of appreciating my best licks as a writer. In other words, I would have written *down* to the audience.

What I have learned over the years, performing my stories in front of hundreds of thousands of kids, is that they are much more perceptive than I ever dreamed. Every child might not catch every word or every joke, but even the little ones seem to understand the characters.

This never ceases to amaze me, because Hank is not a simple character. Consider, for example, that everything the reader knows about the story, he learns from Hank, the narrator. *And Hank lies!* He's always feeding the reader misinformation and disinformation, stretching the truth, and trying to conceal his mistakes.

That is pretty subtle, and I wouldn't have thought that kids would be sharp enough to catch it, but they do. They seem to have an intuitive grasp of Hank's character. They take delight in watching him wind himself up in a web of silly lies. They forgive him for stretching the truth, because they know that he has a good heart.

I'm still not sure how the kids discovered the Hank stories. It was just something that happened on its own. At Maverick Books we did nothing to promote or advertise the books to a young audience. But by the fall of 1985 we were getting calls from teachers and librarians: "Our children are bringing these Hank the Cowdog books to school, and they're passing them around. What is Hank the Cowdog and who is John Erickson, and does he ever do programs in schools?"

And that's how I learned that I had become an author of children's books. My audience told me what I was supposed to be doing.

CHAPTER FOUR

SELF-PUBLISHING

"One thing true artists should never do is to abandon their calling . . .
God's gifts are never to be hidden; his calling is never to be denied."
- Philip Ryken, *Art for God's Sake*

Between 1967 and 1982, I wrote every morning, then went off to jobs that brought in enough money to support my wife and family.

During my writing hours, I often studied novels and charted their plot lines on a roll of butcher paper. *Gone With The Wind* covered three feet of paper and when I had charted every twist and turn of the plot, I had a maze of pencil lines that gave no answer to my question: "What makes this a great story?" Like a dead frog on a dissecting pan, it showed parts but revealed nothing about that mysterious quality we call "life."

I read books on how to write and how to submit a manuscript. I attended writers' conventions and stalked New York editors through hotel lobbies. I sent off query letters by the hundreds, grand ideas for novels, short stories, articles, essays, and plays. I even acquired an agent. It didn't help. Agents, like bankers, serve you best when you really don't need them.

After fifteen years, I had reaped a harvest of rejection slips, probably over a thousand, and the frustration had become unbearable. If God had given me a talent, as my mother used to tell me, why hadn't He informed someone in the publishing business? What was I supposed to do with my talent?

I thought I had good stories to tell and that people needed good stories, yet I couldn't figure out how to make the connection between author and reader. What was I doing wrong? One editor said that the historical novel I'd submitted had "too much integrity and not enough sex" (what do you do with that information?), but the complaint I heard most often was that my work was "too regional."

For years, I responded with anger and tried to argue my case. "Look, all writing is regional, isn't it? We all have to come from somewhere. There was nothing magic about Shakespeare's hometown. Dante was Italian, Goethe was German, Dostoyevsky was Russian, and I'm from rural West Texas. We write about where we are and try to find the universal in the particular."

Ah, how many miles of paper did I roll through my typewriter, arguing the case that all writing is regional? Many miles. But after fifteen years of yelling, arguing, and banging on doors, it finally dawned on me that *publishing is not an argument. It's an expression of power.* When you argue, you've already lost.

The people who pay the printing bill define "good writing," and they don't even have to be right. All they need is enough money to pay the bills. It suddenly struck me that I didn't need the approval of editors, critics, or book reviewers. I needed *readers*, and I thought I could go out and find them.

In September of 1982 I quit my job as a handyman (I had starved out of cowboying the year before), borrowed two thousand dollars from a foolish banker, and started Maverick Books in my garage in Perryton, Texas. Kris and I had two small children, with another on the way. America was going through the worst recession since the Thirties, and I had launched my book business in a town that didn't even have a bookstore.

"Fools rush in . . ."

My first self-published title was *The Devil in Texas and Other Cowboy Tales*, a collection of humorous stories I had written for *The Cattleman* magazine. I needed someone to do illustrations for the book, and knew exactly where to find him. He and his family lived in a little farmhouse two miles north of Perryton.

I had met Gerald Holmes back in 1976, when he was working in a local feedlot and I was cowboying in Oklahoma. The two of us were so poor, we couldn't have come up with the price of a cup of coffee, but when he showed me some of his pen-and-ink drawings of ranch life, I knew that Holmes and I would eventually work together, and six years later, we did.

Holmes had grown up on a ranch near Waurika, Oklahoma, and knew livestock and cowboys to the bone. His drawings were simple, fresh, and funny, and they sparkled with the kind of honesty that comes from first-hand experience. The man could draw a bucking horse, put a face on a dog, and capture the emotions of a ranch wife who has just caught her husband's dog poaching hens in the chicken house. His drawings were a perfect compliment to my stories, and he has illustrated every one of them without ever missing a deadline.

When the first shipment of books arrived in my garage, I went out looking for readers and found them in unusual places. I did programs for any group that would take me, in little agricultural communities within a hundred mile radius of Perryton. I set up a booth at county fairs and rodeos, signed books in saddle shops and western-wear stores, grocery stores, drugstores, and small town banks. I ran ads in livestock magazines and sold through the mail.

I sold books at the National Finals Rodeo and the World Championship Cow Chip-Throwing Contest, and I may be the only author in the United States who has tried to sell books at the livestock auctions in Texhoma, Beaver, and Guymon, Oklahoma. (It's a tough sell. Men who wear overalls and cowboy boots don't buy anything but horse feed and chewing tobacco. Go find their wives.)

But it worked. I sold gentle, funny stories to people who needed gentle, funny stories. A week after my first shipment of 1,500 copies arrived, I ordered a second printing.

In November, I bought an IBM personal computer. At that time, PCs were just coming on the market, and with a price of $5,600, it seemed an extravagant purchase for a small business. But I could see the potential of such a machine, and after talking it over with my father, we decided to buy one. He loaned me the money and I began studying software manuals.

I had to learn three programs at once: a word processor (Word Star, now extinct), a spreadsheet program (Visicalc, the forerunner of Lotus 1-2-3), and a mailing list program. It was frustrating work. The manuals appeared to have been written by foreigners or Martians, and since I was among the first in my town to buy a PC, I had to figure most of it out on my own.

By Christmas, our sales had come to $35,000 and I had hired a lady to help me fill mail and answer the phone, replacing Kris, who had just given birth to our son, Mark. I had finished writing the first book-length Hank adventure. We planned to bring it out the following spring, and I wanted to publish a cassette tape version as well as the book because from the very beginning, the Hank stories were meant to be read aloud.

In 1982, the term "audio book" didn't exist, and I'd never heard of an author recording his own stories but I couldn't afford to hire anyone with talent so I had to figure out how to do it myself. I had done Hank programs for audiences and thought I could do all the voices in the first book, fourteen of them. (There are now over sixty character voices).

Somebody told me that Amarillo had a recording studio, the Audio Refinery, so I called the owner, Dayton Todd, and asked if he'd ever done a book on tape. "Nope." Neither had I. Was he willing to give it a try? "Sure, come on over." So in December of 1982, I walked into a cubicle with padded walls, stepped up to the microphone, and started reading.

After six hours of recording, we had laid down the voice track and Dayton said, "What do you want me to do with this?" I told him to make it sound like an old-time radio program, like the ones I grew up with in the Fifties. After editing out all of my mistakes (he did it manually, cutting and splicing the tape by hand), he added sound effects and background music: chase music, suspense music, and soap opera organ for the romantic scenes.

We brought out the first Hank book, along with the cassette tape version in the spring of 1983. Hank was a popular character from the beginning, and those books were so easy to sell, I wondered if I could write a second Hank book. I gave it a try and knocked out *The Further Adventures of Hank the Cowdog* in two weeks. Kris took the thankless job of being my editor. It seems outrageous that I wrote it so fast, but I had no choice. There was a big nasty wolf howling at my door and I didn't have time to fool around.

By the time we brought out the third Hank book and tape in the spring of 1984, I had decided to write two songs to go with each story on tape. Why not? I was paying the bills and I could do whatever I wanted.

Once again, I had to call upon my own little cluster of talents because I couldn't afford to hire real musicians. I couldn't read or write music, but I played the banjo and had sung in choirs in church and school. My main qualification, though, was that I worked cheap.

I did all the music in the first three episodes, but when I wrote the fourth book, *Murder in the Middle Pasture*, I composed a song that I couldn't play on the banjo. I called it "The Cold Weather Cowdog Blues," and it needed a musician who could play blues piano. It happened that our church had a guest musician about that time, Trev Tevis, a local boy who had taken a music degree at DePaul University and had recently moved back to the family farm.

I don't remember what he played that Sunday morning (it wasn't blues), but I was impressed by the way he took command of the grand piano and used his big hands to squeeze emotion out of the keys. After the service, I asked if he would help me with "The Cold Weather Cowdog Blues," and he said he would give it a try.

Thus began a long and fruitful collaboration, with me composing the songs and Trev doing the arrangements and orchestrations. In the studio, he used a wide variety of instruments: piano, marimba, trombone, tuba, synthesizers, and every kind of percussion instrument known to man. For fifteen years, we traveled thousands of miles in a Suburban, one of us sleeping on a mattress in the back while the other drove. We performed Hank programs in schools all way from the Texas Gulf Coast to Fairbanks, Alaska.

In Fairbanks, we performed "The Cold Weather Cowdog Blues" while several moose stood outside on the school playground, staring at us through the frosted windows.

24

As time went on, I called upon the talents of my wife, Kris. She has a lovely soprano voice and had taught herself to play the mandolin, so we put her to work. As our children grew older, I wrote songs for them and our performances became a family affair. Little Markie began performing in front of an audience when he was four years old and never knew he was supposed to be scared.

For twenty-seven years, we have produced two Hank audios per year, bringing us up to fifty-four. I have been told that it is the longest-running audio series in the United States, and in 1998, we won a national award for the best children's audio book of the year. The audios have found a loyal audience. Hank has helped many a family put children to sleep at night, comforted the sick in hospital rooms, and entertained restless kids on long road trips.

In the spring of 1984, Maverick Books published my biography of famous western cartoonist Ace Reid. With a print run of 13,000 hardbacks, that was a huge project for a small publisher. We also brought out the third Hank episode, and those books continued to sell at a brisk pace. We outgrew our space in my garage and moved to a suite of offices in downtown Perryton where I had four people employed.

We were on a roll and showed all the outward signs of prosperity. *Texas Monthly* magazine called Maverick Books "the most successful self-publishing venture in Texas." Money was flying into the office, but it was also flying out: rent, salaries, new computers, and an inventory that kept growing. I had no formal training in business and couldn't decide whether I was getting rich or going broke, but either way, it was turning into a wild ride.

I began waking up in the middle of the night, seized by the chilling thought that Maverick Books might be heading straight for a cliff, so when a young accounting student from Wayland Baptist University approached me about a summer job, I hired him—and hoped that he could figure out how to squeeze his salary out of our cash flow.

Gary Rinker was a Perryton boy, a tall, quiet, all-state basketball player who had just finished his junior year at Wayland and needed to do a "practicum" to graduate. His mother had taught our son Scot in fourth grade, and his father was an elementary school principal. I knew that Gary was smart, honest, and solid.

He spent the summer in a back room at Maverick Books, going through reports, invoices, and the piles of paper that computers are so adept at churning out. At the end of the summer, he informed me that I was going broke.

I don't remember how I responded. I didn't cry but I'm sure the anger and frustration came pouring out. *How could I be going broke?* I had spent the past two years working fourteen hours a day and doing the jobs of three or four men: writing books, writing songs, recording audios, doing programs, attending autographings, studying computer manuals, filling the mail, running the office, meeting with bankers and accountants, writing ads and news releases, designing catalogs and brochures, calling on stores . . .

What did I have to do to succeed in this business? Young Rinker shrugged. "You have too many employees and too much expense."

I sent Gary back to Wayland with a new Compaq portable computer, and he began doing all the Maverick Books accounting. The following spring, he married Kim, his college sweetheart. They moved to Perryton and Gary went to work as the general manager of Maverick Books. He and a secretary were the only employees. For the first several months, we

26

couldn't afford to pay him a salary. But we survived.

My story throws a harsh light on self-publishing. An author can do everything right and work himself into the ground, but no matter how well he does on the creative side, he still has to succeed in the world of bankers, lawyers, and accountants. And when that banker with the cold blue eyes says, "You're broke," the party is over. If Gary hadn't come along when he did, the saga of Hank the Cowdog might have had quite a different ending.

With Gary running the office, we continued bringing out new Hank titles. In May 1985, CBS Television did a thirty-minute animated cartoon based on the first book, giving us some national exposure—not all of it good. (See Chapter Five.) By then, it was clear, to my astonishment, that Hank was going to be a star and we weren't set up to handle it. We had no sales force and with the ever-growing inventory, our cash flow was tied up in the storeroom.

We decided to approach Texas Monthly Press about taking over the Hank series. We had built up a small but loyal audience and had sold enough copies to make it attractive (75,000). Gary flew down to Austin and negotiated a deal that freed us from the burden of financing the inventory, and for the first time, we started getting royalty checks.

Several years later, Texas Monthly Press was bought by Gulf Publishing Company in Houston. We remained with Gulf until 1998 and pushed the sales of Hank books to 2.5 million copies. At that point, Gulf went through some internal changes, and we decided to shop around for another publisher. We learned that Hank had admirers in New York and moved the series to Viking-Penguin, which has been the publisher of the books ever since.

Maverick Books remains the publisher of the audios (and this book), and we do a good business selling audios, books, and a small line of merchandise to schools, libraries, and individuals, much of it through www.hankthecowdog.com. The internet is a marvelous tool for small businesses.

I never wanted to get into self-publishing, but it has turned out to be the best thing I could have done. It allowed me to write the kind of books I wanted to write—wholesome family entertainment—and to reach the people I care about. Self-publishing allowed us to control the content of the stories and also the subsidiary rights (movies, TV, merchandise, stage plays, music), and to protect the brand from the inertial forces of popular culture. With the standards sinking deeper every year, that has been a blessing.

Hank has become a national character, yet the stories remain what they were at the beginning, when the audience consisted of farm and ranch families in the American heartland. The stories may be "too regional," but they have sold millions of copies and have been translated into Spanish, Danish, Chinese, and Farsi. Maybe "too regional" isn't so bad after all.

Would I recommend self-publishing to other writers?

Yes, but with the caution of an older man who wears scars and knows from experience that there is nothing amusing about unsold boxes of books in the garage. Self-publishing can break your heart and your bank account. I don't know the success-failure ratio, but I'm sure the numbers would be depressing. There are easier ways of losing money, and your odds of winning might be better in Las Vegas.

I went into self-publishing desperate, angry, and ignorant. Every day, for years, I walked through the Valley of the Shadow of Death. If I had made one little misstep, if Gary Rinker hadn't joined the effort, if I hadn't been married to a brave, strong, godly woman, if my parents hadn't advised me and encouraged me, if I hadn't been able to use every little talent I possessed, I might be sweeping out pool halls today.

Our venture should have failed—but somehow it didn't, and that is important information. If we don't approve of the books and movies offered by the establishment media, we have the option of creating something better. It will require the best efforts of brave entrepreneurs and enlightened investors. It won't be easy, but it can be done.

Filmmaker Isaac Botkin has urged young filmmakers to follow a similar course: Learn your craft, write your own screenplays, raise your own money, make your own movies, and stay away from Hollywood, which he describes as "a bottomless pit of nihilism and pessimism." [Botkin 2007:93.] Botkin is trying to do with films what I did with books: Make a good product and go straight to the end-user.

This book marks my return to self-publishing after twenty-one years of following a more conventional path. I chose to publish it myself for several reasons. I considered it a good investment of my own capital. I had no contacts among Christian publishers and didn't want to start all over at the bottom of the ladder, this time trying to prove that I was "Christian enough." I'm too old and grouchy to enjoy such tiresome arguments.

I also had the opportunity to enter into a co-publishing arrangement with Patrick Henry College, a fine Christian school in Virginia. In doing the book ourselves, rather than going through conventional publishing channels, we will give PHC students an opportunity to gain practical experience in the publishing process, including promotion and marketing.

Those are skills that young Christian writers need to acquire, so that when publishing doors are slammed in their faces, they will know how to respond: break it down and keep moving forward.

Finally, I welcomed the opportunity to rediscover the satisfaction of building a finished book out of nothing but dreams and ideas. When self-publishing isn't terrifying, it can be a very exciting adventure.

CHAPTER FIVE

HANK THE COWDOG AND TELEVISION

"There is a death wish inherent in humanism – the impulsive drive
to beat to death the base which made our freedoms and our culture possible."
- Francis Schaeffer, *How Should We Then Live?*

In the summer of 1984, I got a call from a man at CBS Television in Los Angeles. He said they wanted to make a thirty-minute animated cartoon based on one of my Hank the Cowdog books. I was thrilled.

At that time, I was self-publishing the Hank books on borrowed money, selling them out of my garage in the little town of Perryton, Texas, and trying to support a wife and three small children. There couldn't have been more than a few thousand Hank books in the whole world, and I considered it an extraordinary piece of luck that one of them had ended up on a desk in Los Angeles.

Hank was to be one of thirteen episodes, each based on an outstanding children's book, in a series called "CBS Storybreak." The series was part of an attempt by the network to "upgrade" its Saturday morning programming and would be hosted by a trusted name in children's broadcasting, Bob Keeshan, better known as Captain Kangaroo.

The CBS contract gave me no part in writing or approving the script. I didn't like that, but felt I had no choice. I needed the exposure. I signed the contract and hoped for the best.

The Hank episode aired on May 4, 1985, and Perryton was proud. The mayor declared it "Hank the Cowdog Day," and we had a celebra-

31

tion at the same country club where I had spent three years working as a bartender. I watched the Hank episode with two hundred kids from my hometown, including my own: Scot, Ashley, and Mark.

My first impression was that CBS had done a good job with the animation and had stayed pretty close to my story. They missed a lot of the subtlety in Hank's character, choosing to present him as a conventional "good guy," but they captured the dreamy, flighty disposition of his little sidekick, Drover.

I tried to ignore that they had placed Hank on a *chicken farm* instead of a cattle ranch (why do they do things like that?), and that the landscapes resembled the Arizona desert, not the Texas Panhandle. Those changes were annoying but not fatal.

But after watching the episode three times, I noticed something more disturbing. In my book, it is clear that Hank lives on a typical family ranch. Loper and Sally May are husband and wife, and Little Alfred is their son. Slim Chance is a bachelor cowboy who works on the ranch.

In the CBS version, Sally May had become the *ranch boss*. Loper and Slim worked for her and addressed her as "Miss Sally May," and it appeared that they all lived together in the bunkhouse. Little Alfred had vanished into thin air.

I was stunned. *They had taken the family out of my story*!

At first, I thought it must have been an accident (boy, was I naïve!), but then I watched the other episodes in the "Storybreak" series and noticed that in all thirteen of these "high quality" stories for children, only one showed a traditional family with a husband and wife.

What was going on here? I hadn't read the other books in the series, but I knew what they'd done to my story. They had removed all traces of the kind of home life that had been a source of strength to me, my parents, my grandparents, and back as far as we could trace our family history.

Why had they done this? I could only conclude that someone at the network had decided to use a Saturday morning cartoon series, and my Hank book, as a platform for a secular ideology that viewed women as an oppressed minority, men as brutes, marriage as slavery, and motherhood as a waste of time.

They had politicized my innocent, funny little story . . . and they had done it by stealth.

I was particularly outraged because my Hank stories were always meant to be read aloud by *families*. If the television people felt contempt for two-parent families, why hadn't they chosen a book that *said so*, out in the open, where everyone could see it?

The reason, I suspect, is that such books don't exist, or, if they do, they've become spectacular flops in the marketplace. What kind of parents would give such a book to their child for Christmas? What kind of teacher would read it aloud to her fourth-grade class? What kind of librarian would recommend it to the children in her care?

Feminist crusaders can't produce their own children's books, because *nobody trusts them*. Deep instinct tells us that anyone who hates the traditional two-parent family doesn't like children either. To them, children are noisy, messy little animals who interfere with a woman's busy career . . . though feminists don't seem to mind selling soda pop, sugared cereal, and toys to children who have no defense against the psychological assaults of television advertising.*

So they buy the rights to a successful book by a trusted author and inject it with their social viruses.

What qualifies these people to indoctrinate our children? Where is the proof that broken homes are a proper setting for nurturing children and passing along civilized values? There is no proof. None. In six thousand years of recorded history, no group of human beings has ever been arrogant enough or drunk enough to argue such hideous rubbish, yet every day in modern America, someone is beaming that message into our homes. Sometimes it's out in the open. More often, it's hidden, disguised like a thief in the night.

When I made my deal with CBS, I never dreamed they would use my story as a vehicle for undermining the ethics of my parents, church, and community. I'm ashamed that I was such an easy mark. I got whipped because I didn't know I was in a fight.

---

*A friend who read this book in manuscript pointed out that feminist crusaders do write books for children, and they do get them published. They don't sell many copies but often win prestigious national awards bestowed by judges who share their worldview.

Chapter Six

Disney

"Entertainment media illustrates the theology of our culture."
- Isaac Botkin, *Outside Hollywood*

In 1985 I attended a book-and-author affair in Ft. Worth and made the acquaintance of a man I'll call James Milburn. He was a pleasant fellow and showed an interest in my writing. Originally from the East Coast, he was trying to establish himself as a literary agent in Texas and wondered if I would be interested in using his services.

I explained that I had used agents in the past, four or five of them, and nothing had ever come of it. He said he wanted to make some calls in my behalf. If nothing worked out, I owed him nothing.

Over the following year, we became friends. When business took me to Austin, I stayed overnight with him and his wife. We spent many pleasant hours out on his patio, talking about the problems Texas authors faced in dealing with New York publishers and Hollywood studios. James wanted to find a home for some western novels I had written, but his primary interest lay in the Hank the Cowdog series, which he felt had tremendous potential as a franchise of animated movies.

From the very beginning, Kris and I had thought so, too, and so had Gary Rinker when he joined us. Anyone who had grown up with the classic Disney movies, as I had, could hardly escape the feeling that, in the right hands, the Hank stories could be made into a beautiful series of animated movies, the kind of films entire families could watch and enjoy.

Although the Hank episode on CBS television had been flawed, it had given us a bit of credibility. James thought he could build on that and said he had contacts at Hanna-Barbera and Disney. I liked James but doubted that he had much influence in California, so I was surprised when he called in July 1986 and said he'd had a good conversation with a man named Robert at Disney Pictures. Robert had read *Murder in the Middle Pasture,* the fourth Hank book, and liked it. He wanted to talk to me.

The next day, I called him. He said he loved my writing style, language, and characters, but thought my books were too short and too "episodic" for a feature film. He wondered if I could write up a "story concept" with a broader conflict. He couldn't make any promises, but if he liked it, Disney might offer a contract and pay me to work on a story "treatment," the next step between a concept and a screenplay. I told him I would give it a try.

When I hung up the phone, my head was filled with songbirds and butterflies. I couldn't have wished for anything bigger or better than working with Disney to make the kind of family movies Walt and his animators were making in the late 1930s and early 1940s. Wow! I rushed to find Kris and told her the news, then spent the rest of the afternoon and evening watching Disney movies on video tape, making notes as I watched.

The next morning, I went to my office (a little apartment above our garage) at 2:30, instead of the usual 5:30, and started working on a story concept that I hoped would fit Robert's description of a "bigger story." The following morning, I finished it, printed it out, and sent it to James Milburn, express mail. Then I started working on a second story concept.

I had gotten so excited about Disney, I found it hard to sleep—and that has never worked well for me. After three days of frenetic activity, I coasted to a stop and finally got a good night's sleep.

While waiting to hear something from Disney and James Milburn, I drove to the nearest bookstore (in Amarillo, 120 miles away) and bought every book I could find on the subject of Walt Disney and the Disney Studio. It happened that Disney's latest animated movie, "The Great Mouse Detective," was showing at a theater in Amarillo, so I went to see it.

This film appeared to contain the main ingredient that Robert had talked about, a "big story" that followed the three-act template of screenplay design. The right things happened at the right time, the story turned when it was supposed to turn, and everything fit into place. The animation was what you would expect from Disney: lush, the best money could buy.

It was a masterpiece of technique, but it struck me as a shell without a heart. They had put their "big story" on the screen and all it lacked was a set of characters that I cared about. I found most of them cold and not particularly likeable, and I had difficulty even remembering their names.

In other words, story technique dominated the movie and pushed the characters into the places they were required to occupy, speaking lines that would propel the "big story" toward a conclusion. When the script called for a song, they did their duty and burst into song. The characters seemed to have become employees of the screenplay, a clear violation of Walt Disney's maxim that story must grow out of character.

This gave me an uneasy feeling about my ability to satisfy the Disney people, because I knew that my Hank stories were character-driven. You could even say that Hank was the story: what he saw, what he *thought* he saw, what he imagined, what he did. If his stories were "episodic," the reason might be that he himself was episodic. He was a dog, after all, not an actor dressed up in a dog suit, and *dogs behave in an episodic manner.* That's one of the reasons we find them so funny.

Back in Perryton, I devoured my new books on Disney and started keeping a notebook of reading notes and story ideas. The more I learned about Walt Disney, the man, the more convinced I became that he would have been able to make a beautiful movie out of the Hank stories . . . but what about the people who had taken over the Dream Machine after his death in 1966?

If they wanted a big story about "important" conflicts, my Hank the Cowdog might never fit the role, because 99% of time, what Hank does is not important at all, although he doesn't know it. It's funny but not anything that would make the evening news. If you forced Hank into doing things that were "important," you created a different character and the magic in the book-Hank might very well disappear. The story would overpower the character.

Weeks passed, then on August 10, I got a call from James Milburn. When I heard him singing the Mickey Mouse song through the phone, I figured it was a prelude to good news. He said that Robert had presented the Hank material to the head of Disney Pictures (Jeffrey Katzenberg), and he liked it. Robert had gotten the okay to move along to the next step and wanted us to fly out to California and spend several days. Disney would pay for everything.

To say that this phone call created a stir of excitement around our house would be an understatement. I was so excited, I wanted to run down the middle of Main Street, shouting the news.

On August 20, I drove to the airport in Amarillo to catch an early flight to the West Coast. As I approached the airport, I noticed that the odometer on my car turned 100,000 miles, reminding me that this would be a very good time for Hank to provide us with a new source of income. Kris and I had been married for nineteen years and had never faced a day without money worries. The car I was driving, a hand-me-down from my father, was the latest in a long string of clunkers we had driven over the years, and its days were surely numbered.

Maybe crossing the one hundred thousand mile threshold would prove to be a good omen.

When I arrived at the Los Angeles airport, James Milburn was there, having flown in from Austin. We took a cab to the Disney Studios on Buena Vista Drive in Burbank, where a young lady gave us a private tour of the fabled Dream Factory. We saw the new archives building, the sound stage, and back lot. This was a huge operation, a small town within the city of Burbank. It had its own police force and fire department, and even had a lumber yard that was almost as big as the one in my hometown.

From there, we drove over to Flower Street, where the animation people were housed in an unmarked, nondescript building. There was no emblem of The Mouse on the front or anything else to alert passing tourists that this was where the magic was born. It could have been a warehouse or a mattress factory.

There, our tour guide passed us on to Robert and said good-bye. Robert appeared to be in his early thirties, wore a thin black beard, and dressed in a casual manner, including loafers with no socks. I found him friendly and courteous, though a bit distant. He told us that he had been trained as an animator, in a college program set up and endowed by Disney. He now held a management position in the animation department and had worked on *The Great Mouse Detective*.

In our tour of the animation division, Robert introduced me to several of his artists. They already knew the Hank stories and seemed genuinely pleased to meet me. One of them said, "Those characters are so vivid, they almost draw themselves." On our way out of the building, we passed a man with a thin black mustache. Robert called out, "Roy, I want you to meet someone." Roy Disney, Jr., Walt's nephew, came over and shook my hand. He was cordial, but I got the impression that he had never heard of me or Hank the Cowdog.

Robert drove us to a sedate Italian restaurant in Glendale, where we were joined by Robert's boss, whom I'll call Paul Lawrence, the head of the animation division. I was struck at once by his youthful appearance. I wouldn't have guessed that he'd had time to advance to such an important position. His thin face was dominated by intense blue eyes. During the meal, when others were talking, I sensed that he was studying me, and when we spoke to each other, he held me in a wide unblinking gaze that revealed an agile mind and a keen intellect.

We spent the first half hour getting acquainted, then Paul said, "Well, shall we talk about Hank? John, we like the stories but don't know what to do with them." When I asked him to explain exactly what he was looking for in a story, he said, "Frankly, we don't know. If we did, we wouldn't have brought you out here. We would have generated the story in-house, the way we've always preferred doing it."

He admitted that he wasn't pleased with any of their recent pictures (including *The Great Mouse Detective*) and wanted to tell the kind of stories Walt was doing in the 1940s—*Peter Pan* and *Cinderella*, stories that were based on fables. "But you shouldn't try to imitate what Disney has done in the past. We want the story you want to tell."

As we were leaving the restaurant, Paul gave me a bit of a warning. "You should know that in the movie business, the writer is the least important element."

James Milburn, my agent, considered the meeting a success. He and Paul had worked out a schedule for the next two days, allowing James to meet with Disney's legal people. He thought that by the time we flew back to Texas, we would be close to some kind of deal.

I wasn't so sure the meeting had been a success. I still didn't have a firm idea of the kind of story they wanted. The conversation had left me confused. They weren't satisfied with *The Great Mouse Detective*, yet it appeared that they wanted me to put Hank into the same kind of big-story equation. I still had the feeling that Hank's character would get lost in the scramble to make a big, "important" story.

The next day, while James was meeting with the Disney lawyers, I had a script conference with Robert and Paul, and we discussed the story concepts I had submitted. They felt that my concepts missed the mark. They showed a different style than the one in the books. The story concepts seemed "imposed" and lacked "casualness" of the books. Hank didn't seem to be driving the story forward.

Paul asked if I had seen *Witness* with Harrison Ford. I had not. "We'll arrange for you to have a private showing in our theater. It's a good story, where two worlds collide. That's the kind of story we're looking for. We want to see the collision of two worlds and find out what happens."

That afternoon, I sat alone in the studio's private theater, which was almost as large as the Ellis Theater in my hometown, while a man in the projection booth ran *Witness*. Two hours later when the house lights came on, I asked myself, "Was it a good movie? Did I like it?"

41

On the technical side, it was a good movie (Harrison Ford didn't make many bad ones), but I couldn't shake the feeling that to achieve the "collision of worlds," the script writers had cheapened a community of simple Amish farmers by exposing them to the ugliness and brutality of urban postmodern America. The writers had dumped nitro and glycerin into the same beaker and had gotten the big bang they wanted, but when the story ended, what was left to celebrate?

John Book, the Harrison Ford character, had survived the collision of worlds and proved himself a man of courage, satisfying the requirements of the "big story" formula, but to win his status as a hero, he had spilled blood on Amish soil (they are gentle people, pacifists) and bedded down an Amish widow in her father's barn.

Somehow, it reminded me of a story I'd heard about a friend's bird dog. "He jumped into the neighbor's yard, bred all the females, ate all the food, and left, feeling very proud of himself."

When John Book drove off into the sunset, I felt as though he had left Eden infected with smallpox—a personal triumph for him and the screenplay, a tragedy for a community of honest Christian farmers. Maybe that was the whole point of the film, that simple piety can't survive in a secular world, and maybe I wasn't sophisticated enough to accept that as a satisfactory ending.

Above all, though, I couldn't imagine any "collision of worlds" that would allow Hank to be himself.

I walked out of the theater feeling lonely and perplexed. I didn't know it at the time, but *Witness* had exposed a collision of worldviews that went beyond the screenplay. It was a collision between the worldview embedded in the fabric of my Hank stories and the worldview of contemporary filmmakers. It is a conflict that remains unresolved twenty-three years later.

The next morning, Thursday, I got up at six and worked on a new story treatment. At nine, I had another script conference with Paul and Robert. They asked about *Witness* and I gave a guarded reply. I didn't know what to say. We parted on pleasant terms. I would continue working on story ideas, and they promised to help in any way they could. We all wanted to see Hank in a Disney movie.

On Friday morning, James Milburn had a long meeting with the Disney lawyers and in the afternoon we boarded a plane to Dallas. On the way back to Texas, James gave a positive report about the contract negotiations. They had made good progress on a long list of points. I listened but understood very little of it. Movie contracts are extremely complicated, and most authors don't even try to involve themselves in the negotiating process. That's why we use agents.

If James felt good about the deal, that was all I needed to know. I had my own problems, trying to figure out how to fit Hank into a screenplay that Disney would approve.

Back home, I discovered that the trip to California had drained me of energy. For three days I dragged around the house, taking long naps in the afternoon and accomplishing very little during my writing time in the morning. I had experienced this kind of bone-deep fatigue a few times in the past and had noticed that it followed periods of high intensity and concentration. I had learned to listen to my body, to rest and not argue about it, and that's what I did.

Over the next several months, I continued to work on story ideas, while James and the Disney lawyers argued their way toward a finished contract. He remained cheerful and optimistic. The contract arrived in Saturday's mail, Oct. 24, 1986. I noticed right away that it was a big document, thirty-two legal-sized pages of single-spaced type. The Disney lawyers had sent several copies, so I delivered one to my father and another to Gary Rinker, then went to my office in the garage and began studying the document.

I had read enough real estate, book, and oil-company contracts to know that first readings of legal documents often cause ordinary citizens to experience claustrophobia, but this one seemed to suck the oxygen right out of the room. *It was the most hostile, cold-blooded, predatory contract I'd ever seen*!

I was especially jolted by the clause stating that Disney would be acquiring "all rights to all characters, in all languages, known and unknown, in all parts of the universe." Under the contract, Hank the Cowdog would become "Walt Disney's Hank the Cowdog," just as Bambi, the creation of a French author named Salter, became "Walt Disney's Bambi."

I would receive a yet-to-be-determined amount of money, depending upon several contingencies, but my quick calculations suggested that the deal offered only a small sum of hard cash and a lot of blue sky. I would receive NO ROYALTIES from the movie or from any merchandise that accompanied it.

Since the contract dealt with my life's work, I wasn't amused. Neither was my father. He blew a gasket. After giving it a quick read, he called me up. "That's a bad contract and you can't sign it!" Gary Rinker, my business partner, agreed.

The next day, I showed it to Doug McGarraugh, a friend who was accustomed to cut-throat contracts in the oil business. After reading it, he cackled, "I thought I'd read bad contracts, but son, this one was written by the Devil!"

He even suggested something I had never considered: The Disney lawyers might be playing defense. "They have no intention of making a movie. They want to put Hank in their vault and get him off the market. With this contract, they can do it for peanuts."

I had several phone conversations with Disney people and pleaded with them to understand that I simply couldn't sign a contract that gave Disney all rights to my life's work and offered me no royalties. As reasonable people, couldn't we work out a deal that gave Disney what they wanted and allowed me to share in the income that came from characters I had created?

Their answer was a polite "no." Disney had a policy of not paying royalties to authors. (The only exception to that, as far as I know, came in their dealings with the author of *Mary Poppins*. Walt wanted to do the story and gave ground). The position of their legal department was that they had worked up a deal with my agent and I could either sign it or not.

I was stunned when James Milburn recommended that I sign it. It destroyed my faith in his judgment and we parted company.

Obviously, James had waded into waters that were way over his head. Like me, he had spent his college years in the arts and sciences department, reading English novels and writing ponderous essays about Plato's *Republic*. Like me, he had no background in law or accounting. To become a literary agent, he had passed no test or received any kind of certification but had merely decided that he was qualified to make deals in the entertainment business.

He might have done all right, negotiating a standard book contract, but movie deals were something quite different, involving several stages of development, and layer upon layer of obligations and compensation. Without consulting an entertainment lawyer or accountant, he had tried to negotiate with one of the most ferocious legal departments in the Western Hemisphere, a lamb among wolves. Nobody on the Disney-side had bothered to tell him that they loved lamb chops.

James was a clever man, witty and intelligent, a natural mimic who could entertain a crowd, telling stories in accented voices and doing amazing impressions of characters who spoke broken French, Spanish, Italian, or Russian. In fact, he spoke none of those languages, but he had a talent for convincing people that he did. That talent led him into places where he shouldn't have gone.

But even if James had had a stronger background in entertainment law, I'm not sure we could have gotten the kind of deal I wanted. The Disney Corporation had not become a multi-billion dollar enterprise by pampering authors. Without looking too hard, you could find an abundance of stories about authors who had experienced "seller's remorse" about deals they had signed with Disney. Ace Reid, the Texas cartoonist, told me that after his friend Fred Gipson signed the rights to *Old Yeller* over to Disney, he went into a depression that lasted for months.

The public rarely saw this side of the Disney Corporation. Uncle Walt was a genius at public relations, portraying himself as the friend of animals and children. The nasty work went on behind the scenes, where the other Disney brother, Roy Sr., handled all the business that involved bankers, lawyers, accountants, unions, and authors. There was never any doubt that Roy Disney Sr. played hardball. He was a tough cookie, and though he had passed on long before I got there, the tradition continued.

DISNEY

In January 1987, I had my last phone conversation with Paul Lawrence. He said, "We certainly don't want you to sign a contract you don't like. Maybe you should submit your own contract and let us look at it. In any event, keep in touch. We want to do this movie."

Over the next four months, Gary Rinker had several conversations with people in Disney's legal affairs department, and we read contract revisions until we almost went blind. By the summer, the phone calls had become fewer and farther apart, and then they stopped. Without a bang or even much of a whimper, our hopes of making a Hank movie with Disney just faded away.

It was a sad turn of events, and I couldn't help feeling some bitterness. From my perspective, Disney's position was unreasonable and shortsighted (the word "greedy" came to mind), but business deals are ultimately decided on the basis of self-interest and we must assume that the decision-makers at Disney felt that they could get along just fine without Hank.

And they did. In the 1990s, Disney went on to make a string of animated features that found huge success at the box office (*The Lion King, The Little Mermaid,* and others) and made a fortune in the merchandising business that followed each movie. These stories were generated in-house, the way the studio had always preferred doing it, and they didn't have to split the royalty income with an outside writer.

The other side is that we didn't do badly ourselves. Twenty-three years later, we are still bringing out two new Hank titles each year and are still making an honest living, selling one book at a time. And I still control the movie, television, and merchandising rights.

If we had reached a compromise with Disney's legal department

47

and signed a contract, I might very well have been disappointed with any movie they made. In the two decades following our discussions with Disney, the corporation aroused considerable anger in pro-family, pro-Christian, and pro-conservative circles over a substantial track record indicating that Disney had drifted away from the moral sensibility that Uncle Walt had always put into his films.

His worldview was never openly Christian, yet it bore a strong resemblance to the kind of small town, culturally Christian worldview he knew as a boy in the Midwest. The Disney Corporation of today is no slave to Walt's pro-family, Christian-friendly "Main Street Morality," and some critics would say they have become hostile to it. In other words, Hank and "post-Walt" Disney might not have turned out to be the perfect match I thought they were in 1986.

It is clear to me now that neither James nor I was equipped to do business or battle with a major studio. The big literary agencies that *were* qualified to do business at that level had fortified themselves against inquiries from authors just like me, obscure, unpublished or self-published writers who had a big dream and a story that would "make the next blockbuster movie." If I had tried to approach them, I doubt that they would have even answered my phone calls, and by then I was tired of begging.

James and I found each other because we were both trying to scratch out a living on the edges of an industry dominated by big corporations. He got me in the front door at Disney, something I couldn't have done myself, but once there, he got bushwhacked. I always liked James and considered him a friend, but he was a man who didn't know his limits or fear his own inexperience.

Maybe things turned out as they should have, proving once again that some of God's greatest gifts are unanswered prayers.

- PART TWO -

FAITH, CULTURE, AND THE CRAFT OF WRITING

CHAPTER SEVEN

WRITING AS A VOCATION

"God has chosen to work through human beings, who, in their different capacities and according to their different talents, serve each other. This is the doctrine of vocation."
- Gene Edward Veith, *God at Work*

I tell aspiring authors that they should have some experience at living life before they try to write about it. They should pursue activities that are likely to involve the basic elements of story material—characters, relationships, conflict, adventure. In my case, I spent eight years working as a ranch cowboy and later operated my own ranch in the Texas Panhandle. Still do.

Those experiences have given me a solid background from which to draw story material, and they also have prevented me from becoming in-grown, which is one of the hazards of the writing business. But beyond that, I must admit that I don't know where stories come from, why one person finds a diamond and another finds only a pile of gravel. The creative process remains a mystery to me, even though I'm involved with it every day.

What I do know, and have learned over a long career, is that if I follow certain patterns of behavior, I am able to write at least two good books per year—not just two books but two *good* books. For twenty-seven years I have knocked on Hank's door, and so far, he has always appeared.

A disciplined approach to writing is an important part of the process. I write every morning, rain or shine, summer or winter, for no more than four and a half hours. I have learned that if I go beyond four and a half hours, my writing shows fatigue. For me, writing is a long distance race, not a sprint, so endurance is a quality I cultivate.

This puts me at odds with the popular notion that the artist is supposed to be a tormented genius—a Strindberg, Nietzsche, or Ezra Pound who goes mad for his art. American popular music has produced an entire pantheon of musicians who used artificial means to sustain their creativity and went to dark places to find inspiration. I never saw the appeal of dying young or thought that art was worth the sacrifice.

Another element in my writing discipline is that I stopped reading fiction in 1983, after I had written the second Hank book and realized that the Hank stories would become a series. This decision formed a kind of dividing line between Before Hank and After Hank. In the Before Hank years, I read a great deal of fiction and tried to mimic the style of every writer as I searched for the proper literary vehicle to express the things I wanted to say.

The amazing thing about the Hank stories is that they came without effort. I wasn't looking for Hank, trying to imitate another writer, or chasing an idea about story construction. The pattern just fell into my lap, like a gift: an opening line ("It's me again, Hank the Cowdog."), twelve chapters per book, seven double-spaced pages per chapter, and a closing line ("Case closed"), narrated by a ranch dog in Texas who has very little self-knowledge.

Since I couldn't attribute the success of the Hank stories to my own cleverness, I became almost superstitious about protecting the process that had produced them. It occurred to me that my job was to write stories, not to be an expert on children's literature or literature in general. Some authors can do both (C.S. Lewis comes to mind), but I feared that my habit of trying to mimic other writers might spoil the gift I had received.

I feared the natural human tendency to want more than we deserve. Let's say that you receive a check in the mail for a thousand dollars—unexpected, out of nowhere. For two hours, you're ecstatic. "Wow, a thousand bucks!" But then you find yourself thinking, "Only a thousand bucks? Ten thousand would have been so much better."

This has been a theme in several of the Hank stories. In *The Case of the Midnight Rustler*, Hank goes camping with Slim Chance, the cowboy. At dusk, Slim builds a fire and cooks himself a supper of fried potatoes and weenies. Hank has to watch him eat, and the longer he watches, the more he wants to eat a hot dog.

He notices that the package of weenies is sitting on a rock nearby, and that Slim is so preoccupied with his supper, he isn't paying attention. Hank sticks his nose into the package and sniffs. "Oh, wonderful weenie! Just one, that's all I needed." He eats one and it's so delicious, he decides to eat another. And another. Before he knows it, he has eaten the entire package of weenies.

Does it bring satisfaction? Yes, for a few minutes, then (we knew this was coming) he gets sick and burps garlic for the rest of the night, so miserable that he can't sleep. The audiobook version of this scene is very funny. Carlos Casso, the sound engineer and producer of the Hank audios, used his entire library of prerecorded belches to capture the mood.

How much is enough? What does it take to bring satisfaction? That is a constant problem for Hank . . . and for humans, too. As a writer, I hoped to avoid spoiling what I had received (the gift of Hank) by wanting more, and I stopped reading fiction so that I wouldn't be tempted.

My approach to writing has not been dramatic or romantic. It draws upon practical wisdom from ranching: Don't pump your water well so hard that it gocs dry; don't overgraze your pastures; don't milk your cow so often that she drops dead.

The model I use in my writing is not the tormented genius screaming back at the storm, but a mule pulling a plow, around and around, hour after hour and day after day. Pulling a plow is a mule's *vocation*. Mine is writing good stories for people who need good stories. (See Gene Edward Veith's discussion of the doctrine of vocation in Veith 2002 and Veith 2008:151ff.)

This "vocational model" requires that I go through certain rituals to prepare my mind and spirit for the task of telling stories that will benefit the reader. I follow a regular pattern that includes eating nourishing meals (my wife is an excellent cook and nutritionist), doing physical labor on my ranch, getting adequate rest, and maintaining harmonious relationships with my wife and family.

I must spend time in solitude, attend worship services at our church, sing in the church choir, play my banjo, listen to certain types of music (classical sacred, contemporary Christian, and some bluegrass), read and study the Bible, participate in the life of my hometown (a lot of weddings and funerals), and observe the behavior of animals, especially dogs.

There are other things I try to avoid: fast food, meetings, cocktail parties, television, movie theaters, advertising, and music that is loud, dissonant, or depressing. I try to control my daily intake of what we refer to as "information." Conventional wisdom holds that we need more information, but I don't agree.

The electronic age can overwhelm us with images. Some of it might pass as information but much of it is noise. It appears to me that the average one-hour news broadcast contains about six minutes of information and fifty-four minutes of noise. (In *The Screwtape Letters*, the devil Screwtape boasts, "We will make the whole universe noise in the end.") [Lewis 2002:249]

Screening out the noise of popular culture is an important part of my preparation as an author. I do my writing in a small office near my home, and we might describe it as a "sensory-deprived environment." It has no television, radio, CD player, telephone, or internet access, not even a magazine or newspaper. I have no mirror or pictures on the walls.

Beside me on a shelf sits a human skull that I bought forty years ago in an open-air market in Mexico City. It reminds me that "All men are like grass and all their glory is like the flowers of the field. The grass withers and the flowers fall" (1 Peter 1:24, NIV). It reminds me that I have work to do and the clock is running.

I try to avoid any substance or stimulus that raises my blood pressure, gives me a headache, interrupts my sleep, causes me to want things I shouldn't want, or allows me to forget that I am part of God's creation.

We might compare my efforts to cultivate the creative process to a gardener's management of a compost heap. Composting is a process that turns organic waste products into fertile soil. Over a period of months, the gardener tosses grass cuttings, dried leaves, and the peelings of potatoes, carrots, apples, and oranges into a pit.

There it remains and decomposes until the individual parts dissolve and blend into a rich mixture that can be applied on a garden plot, where it nourishes plants that produce vegetables that nourish the family of the gardener.

People who tend compost heaps are fanatical about what goes into them. It must be organic material, never garbage that might include solvents, plastic, paper with ink or dye, or inorganic substances that might be harmful.

What you put into your compost heap is *what you eat*. This is chemistry at its most basic level, also known as nutrition. If you give your compost heap garbage, it gives you garbage back.

The same principle applies to the creative process. I never know exactly what will come out of my mental/spiritual compost heap. The characters, dialog, and plot lines that end up in my stories bear some resemblance to the experiences I've had, yet they've been transformed in mysterious ways into something else. But the important thing is that *they don't become toxic.*

A tormented genius sees himself as an isolated individual, laboring to satisfy his own personal needs. I look at myself as a part of several communities that form a whole network of overlapping vocations. I am an author, but also a husband to my wife, a father to my children, a grandfather to my grandchildren, a rancher in a small community of ranchers, a member of a church, and a citizen of the United States.

All those living relationships contribute to my work as an author, and if I fail at one of them, it is difficult or impossible for me to succeed in my vocation as an author. Francis Schaeffer is right: "Even for the great artist, the most crucial work of art is his life." [Schaeffer 1973:33]

There is a direct and vital link between my vocation as author and my wife's vocation as wife, mother, and keeper of the home. Her vocation strengthens me as a man, and what she does in her kitchen is very similar to what I hope to accomplish in my writing office.

Kris is a serious, life-long practitioner of the art and craft of food preparation. The word "cook" describes only a small part of what she does. She reads books and magazines that deal with nutrition and body chemistry. She knows the nutritional needs of every member of her family. She has a whole library of cookbooks and exchanges recipes with other women. Her spice cabinet is large and she grows some of the herbs in her garden.

She spends time preparing menus and shopping for fresh ingredients, then takes care to see that they are well preserved in her walk-in pantry, two deep freezes, and large refrigerator. Sometimes she uses special methods that require knowledge, skill, and time, such as canning, freezing, and making jelly from the juice of wild plums that grow on our ranch. For my great-grandparents, pioneer ranchers in West Texas, wild plumb juice was their only source of vitamin C.

She spends a great deal of time cleaning the raw ingredients, cutting, trimming, dicing, and parboiling. She makes sauces and blends spices, filling the house with tantalizing smells. When she puts the meal on the table for her family, for a cowboy crew, or for a gathering of friends, it is safe (no tainted ingredients), nutritious, and pleasing to the taste.

Kris sees cooking as part of her vocation as wife, mother, and keeper of the home, and it's not just a job. It's a Christian calling, and her preparation actually begins in the early morning, when she spends quiet hours studying the Bible, planning her day, and thinking about her role in the larger scheme of things.

This is a vital step, because if there is no connection between her labors, her humanity, and God's plan, then the entire process loses whole-ness and meaning. Cooking becomes what the feminists believe it to be: drudgery and servitude.

Can we say that a fine meal is somehow "Christian?" I think we can. Food preparation brings people and families together (as the early Christians did), strengthens bodies (the body is God's temple), and per-mits us to enjoy God's creation through our senses of smell and taste. The beauty of taste is directly related to the chemistry of nutrition. "There can be no question. God is interested in beauty. God made people to be beau-tiful. And beauty has a place in the worship of God." [Schaeffer 1973:26]

The beauty in good stories should have a parallel effect. Good stories should nourish the spirit, just as a good meal nourishes the body.

Feminists have done their best to denigrate the role of women as preparers of food, mocking it as nothing but domestic slavery. When a woman spends hours every day preparing meals for her family, it is, they believe, meaningless work that degrades her as a person.

The feminist argument arises from a secular worldview that defines womanhood in strictly economic and political terms. It does not recognize the existence of anything sacred or holy, except perhaps an unlimited right to decide who in the womb lives or dies. It has no concept of vocation or servant-hood. It places a woman at the center of a universe where her needs and desires are the only things that matter.

That same secular worldview has inflicted the same type of spiri-tual damage to my profession, writing. In both cases, the practitioner of a craft has been cut off from any concept of vocation—serving others to fulfill God's plan. If there is no plan for us to follow, then "nutrition" for the human spirit seems an empty concept, and it really doesn't matter what we eat or what we read.

We are free to believe that the preparation of food is meaningless work and free to trust our body chemistry to strangers, but we pay a terrible price. The effects of unhealthy art, literature, and entertainment are not as obvious as the effects of commercial fast-food, but we can find them in broken marriages, broken homes, broken lives, and broken dreams.

Should a writer care whether his stories help make readers better or worse, strong or weak, sick or healthy? I think we should.

CHAPTER EIGHT

CULTURE AS AN EXPRESSION OF RELIGIOUS FAITH

"Despite the differences among them, all major civilizations have believed in a divine order that lays down the law for both natural and human realms."
- Pearcey, Fickett, and Colson, *How Now Should We Live?*

"The fool hath said in his heart, 'There is no God.'" - Psalms 14:1

Writers spend a lot of time working alone, but we also belong to communities: a family, a town, a school, a church, a state, and the American nation. Our stories have an effect on those communities, making them better or worse, stronger or weaker.

We are more than solitary individuals and have a strong investment in the spiritual/intellectual environment that often goes by the term "Western Civilization," which we might define as the "classical heritage from Greece and Rome, combined with the biblical heritage of Jews and Christians." [Veith 2008:120]

As I understand it, civilization begins with a system of religious thought that defines heaven and earth, man and God, good and evil. If it acquires the protection of a state and an army, as Christianity did during the reign of Constantine, it can flower into a culture that expresses its highest visions through art, sculpture, architecture, literature, and music.

For artistic people, the culture is the air we breathe and the sunlight that gives life to our work. It expresses a worldview that defines who we are, where we came from, and what we should do while we're on this earth.

60

It is also the ultimate source of story technology. A story "lives" because it moves, and it moves back and forth between our concepts of right and wrong. Without a sense of right and wrong that is shared by a whole community, a story doesn't function.

Right and *wrong* are objective but not neutral concepts. They are highly charged fields of thought that emerge from the incubator of culture—religious faith, or what you might call the ultimate presuppositions. That's why it is vital, as Francis Schaeffer writes, that a person's "presuppositions should be chosen after a careful consideration of what worldview is true." [Schaeffer 1985:84]

For me, that faith is rooted in the Protestant Christian worldview, grounded in fact and set forth in the Old and New Testaments. Logic, evidence, and experience have led me to the conclusion that what I do as a storyteller is inexorably linked to that tradition. Without it, my stories don't function and my profession has little meaning or purpose.

Even more important, my profession has no future. I am convinced that a purely secular worldview will poison art at its roots, and without roots it won't survive.

In the first chapter of the Book of Genesis, we find two extraordinary statements: "In the beginning God created the heaven and the earth" (Genesis 1:1) and "So God created man in his own image" (Genesis 1:27).

Those two statements lay the foundation for any expression of culture in the Western world and have profound implications for anyone who is involved in writing or the arts, for as James L. Kugel has pointed out, the first chapter of Genesis lays out the powerful assertion that "our world is fundamentally God's world—everything in it, including ourselves, was made by Him. To say this is more than to report on the origin of things: it is to set out a whole way of perceiving." [Kugel 2007:48]

It says, first, that human life is not the result of chance or random events. We were created by God and are part of an astonishing design that includes everything from subatomic particles to mighty galaxies. Properly done, art should seek out that design, imitate it, amplify it, and translate it into forms that are accessible to the people in our communities. The best of artistic endeavors might even express a sense of reverence and gratitude.

Second, the human spirit is a reflection of our Source. Because we were made in God's image, "a little lower than the angels" and "crowned with glory and honor," (Psalms 8:5), we occupy a special place in the community of creation. We are the only ones that sing, write poetry, and know that we are going to die. Art provides us with a medium for exploring the special nature of our relationship with the Creator. The impulse to create something artistic begins in this blessing of being only a bit lower than the angels.

That sounds very much like something a "Christian writer" might say, yet under most definitions, I don't qualify as one. I have always wanted my books to appeal to the widest possible audience: blacks and whites, young and old, men and women, urban and rural, Southern Baptists, Catholics, Jews, Republicans, Democrats, and everyone in between. Very few religious bookstores carry my Hank books and most Christian publications haven't noticed them.

The fact that the Hank stories have been translated into several languages, including Chinese and Farsi, suggests that what is beautiful and funny to a Christian writer from Texas can cross national, religious, and cultural borders. And I'm delighted.

I built up my audience in the secular environment of the public school system and nobody asked or seemed to care about my faith. I was there because teachers had figured out that kids would read my books. But over the years, the teachers and I began to notice that the stories had a religious *effect*. It was subtle and I have come to describe it as "spiritual nourishment." It isn't overtly Christian, yet when I trace it back to the source, I realize that a Christian worldview is deeply embedded within the fabric of my storytelling.

I think we can establish a kind of statistical grid that offers some clues about the broad characteristics of Christian literature—and notice that it has nothing to do with the repetition of "faith" words, such as God, Jesus, Bible, or Gospel. Christian literature as a total body of work is more likely to be structured than chaotic, more likely to be harmonic than dissonant. It is more likely to find justice, beauty, hope, and resolution than their opposites.

Finally, it should view human life—and the art that seeks to describe it—as a creative effort connected to a larger transcendent vision. "An author should never conceive of himself as bringing into existence beauty or wisdom that did not exist before, but simply and solely as trying to embody in terms of his own art some reflection of eternal Beauty and Wisdom." [Lewis 1995:7]

These qualities (structure, harmony, justice, redemption, hope, wisdom, beauty, and transcendence) are profoundly Christian, but also universally human in their appeal, for all humanity is created in the image of God. You don't have to be Christian to admire the beauty and goodness that arise from a Christian worldview, and we don't have to reduce them to theological propositions in books about articles of faith.

The message is already there, implicit and woven into the fabric of creation and the drama of redemption. It doesn't need to be preached or taught or explained. It needs only to be absorbed.

CHAPTER NINE

WORLDVIEW

"Our choices are shaped by what we believe is real and true, right and wrong,
good and beautiful. Our choices are shaped by our worldview."
- Pearcey, Fickett, and Colson, *How Now Should We Live?*

Worldview conflicts have been around for a long time. During the reign of King Henry VIII of England, William Tyndale was branded a heretic, tied to a stake, and strangled to death. His crime: translating the Bible into English, the vernacular of the common man. Tyndale and the Roman Catholic Church had a serious difference of opinion on worldview. [Farris 2007:37]

My worldview problem with CBS Television wasn't as serious as Tyndale's (I got mugged, he got strangled), but it was serious enough. At the time my story aired on national television, I had never heard the term "worldview" and didn't even realize that I had one—a shocking revelation, since I'd spent two years at Harvard Divinity School—or that the television people had one, too. Or that my worldview and theirs might be very different. But as Francis Schaeffer and other writers have pointed out, every piece of writing, every movie, every work of art contains a worldview.

Mine traces back to the small town in rural West Texas where I grew up. It contains the social norms of a group of people who till the soil, tend livestock, and operate small businesses. We pay our bills on the tenth of every month, believe in thrift, personal honesty, fidelity in marriage, hard work, and the importance of being good parents. We don't always live up to our principles, but at least we think we should.

65

Our lives center around work, school, family, and church, and our system of ethics derives from the Bible that William Tyndale translated into English. It was Tyndale's wish to make the Scriptures available to the average citizen ("ploughman," to use his term), and the people in my community are a close match to his "ploughman."

The Hank cartoon that appeared on national television expressed a different worldview, a brand of secular thought that could probably be traced back to the writings of Marx, Freud, Nietzsche, Darwin, and Rousseau. The people who altered my story might have thought they were improving it, scrubbing out a backwoods approach to marriage and family.

Or maybe they weren't even aware of what they were doing. But they did it anyway, changing my story at a fundamental level and removing all traces of the biblical two-parent family. It taught me a painful lesson about the power of worldview.

Last December, I participated in an event that captured my vision of what can happen when a Christian worldview expresses itself through the medium of art. The small community in which I grew up, and to which I still belong, is remarkable in that, every December for the past fifty years, we have performed the Christmas portion of Handel's *Messiah*. Kris and I have sung in the community chorus since we moved to Perryton in 1970. Two of our children sang in the chorus when they were in high school.

The service was held in the sanctuary of the First United Methodist Church where Kris and I have been members for thirty years. Ours is a beautiful church whose architecture invokes an attitude of worship. It has been called "Cathedral of the Plains" because of its vaulted ceiling and splendid stained glass windows. For decades we've had a strong music program (choir, piano, and pipe organ) that adds the harmony of sound to the harmony of space, affirming "a personal God who created structures of beauty in the very texture of the universe." [Veith 1991:37]

By six o'clock, the sanctuary was filled, even the balcony, and a hush spread through the crowd as the string ensemble from the Amarillo Symphony took their places and began playing. Looking out at the crowd, I recognized people I had known over a lifetime. I had autographed their Hank books, watched their boys play football on Friday night, and attended the weddings and funerals of their loved ones.

I saw Methodists, Nazarenes, Mennonites, Disciples of Christ, Presbyterians, Catholics, members of the Church of Christ, five varieties of Baptists, and members of small non-denominational churches whose names are hard to remember. I saw farmers, ranchers, accountants, lawyers, doctors, nurses, police officers, housewives, merchants, teachers, homeschoolers, oil field workers, truck drivers, and firemen, all dressed in their finest clothes.

They had come to hear fifty local musicians, most of us of average talent, perform a composition written in 1741 by a German Lutheran living in England.

It was a moving experience for everyone present: the organ, piano, and strings; the chorus, soloists and director; the biblical text, the harmonies, the subtle rhythms . . . all of it blending together inside a sanctuary designed to direct our thoughts to that Source of human creativity higher than ourselves. C.S. Lewis could have had *Messiah* in mind when he wrote:

> When [a musical performance] succeeds, I think the performers
> are the most enviable of men: privileged while mortals to honor

God like angels and, for a few golden moments, to see spirit and flesh, delight and labor, skill and worship, the natural and the supernatural, all fused into that unity they would have had before the Fall. [Lewis 1995:98]

It was a concert and a showcase of local talent, but more than that, it was a service of worship that ennobled the thoughts and nourished the spirits of everyone present. I found myself thinking, "This is art! This is where it begins and this is what it's supposed to do."

That is a sentiment that most of the people in my hometown can understand. The people who made "CBS Storybreak" *don't seem to understand it at all*. And that's the problem.

CHAPTER TEN

STORY STRUCTURE: BEAUTY, JUSTICE, AND FUN

"Good books must be written according
to the aesthetic laws that are part of the created order."
- Gene Edward Veith, *Reading Between the Lines*

Those of us who grew up in Christian homes have been saturated in history and literature written between two and four thousand years ago, and time has not eroded their impact. One of the oldest pieces of written literature known to mankind, "The Epic of Gilgamesh," was recorded on clay tablets some five thousand years ago, yet when we read it today, the story of Gilgamesh and Enkidu still resonates across the ages.

The telling and hearing of stories is part of our legacy as beings who were made in the image of God, "a little lower than the angels" and "crowned with glory and honor" (Psalms 8:5). A good story ought to perform a service by making us better, stronger, wiser, or happier than we were before. It makes us laugh or cry. It imparts wisdom. It teaches lessons about human nature and our place in God's creation. It addresses our need to find coherence in our lives. It gives us a sense of continuity within the overall stream of human experience.

That occurs when writers frame off a piece of experience and describe it well, following the intuitive blueprint inside the human soul that has responded to the craft of storytelling since the dawn of time.

During my apprentice years, no problem caused me more grief than story structure. What is it? Where does it come from? What does it do? Do we even need it? Is there some structure or pattern in human events? If not, writers don't need to fret over story structure or pretend that there might be a difference between a novel and a telephone book. Whatever we scribble down is "a story," and one person's story is as good as the next.

Children see structure in the world around them. It provides coherence from one day to the next. It reveals beauty and meaning. They consider structure normal and take it for granted until, as adults, they are taught that it isn't there. I could never accept that it wasn't there.

At its simplest level, story structure is a frame that we build around experience. It separates certain words and events from all the other words and events in the world, and gives them special significance. Each sentence is built on a pattern, constructed of nouns, verbs, pronouns, adjectives, and adverbs that work together in a common purpose. When we diagram a sentence, it shows the structure of human speech and thought.

Words and events outside the frame might be chaotic and meaningless, but those inside are not.

In the 1980s, I studied William Foster-Harris's book, *The Basic Formulas of Fiction,* in which he argued that most good stories can be reduced to one of four basic plot formulas. Foster-Harris taught a writing course at the University of Oklahoma and guided a number of writers toward successful careers, but I found his formula approach too confining.

Instead, I began imitating models that came from sources outside of literature: folk music and oral-tradition storytelling.

There is symmetry in a folk tune that follows a simple chord progression: G, C, D, and G, for example. G provides the introduction, C creates suspense, and D resolves the tune back to G. It forms a circle, a whole. It has structure. Something inside us responds to the geometry of tone and harmony, and even listeners who don't read or write music can sense it.

Ninety-five percent of all the Anglo-American folksongs ever written (the only tradition I know) can be played with three chords. The remaining five percent add other chords, but the structure of the song remains the same. That doesn't mean we shouldn't experiment with new chords and harmonies. As Francis Schaeffer said of Bach's music, "There can be endless variety and diversity without chaos. There is variety yet resolution." [Schaeffer 1976:92] But we should learn the rules before we try to break them.

Storytellers who operate in an oral tradition follow a pattern that is very similar to the one we find in a folksong, even though they might not be aware of it and probably didn't learn it from a book. They use it because *it works.* Performing in front of a live audience, they can see how listeners respond to a story. If the audience doesn't laugh, falls asleep, or walks out, something is wrong.

Someone who is skilled at telling jokes or stories understands that they are not random utterances. They follow a definite pattern, like a folksong or a sentence that you can diagram. If you follow the pattern, most of the time you get good results. If you ignore the pattern, the joke or story falls flat. The pattern requires movement and resolution.

A novelist who works in isolation doesn't get immediate feedback, but the structure of a written story should contain those same three parts: a beginning or introduction, a period of tension that gives the story its motion, and then a resolution.

In most professions, structure is directly related to function. A good brick wall stands. A good coat fits. A good pot holds water. A good meal nourishes. The structure of a well-built house allows it to resist wind and water. A well-told story should reveal beauty and affirm justice in human experience.

"Beauty" is one of those words we use every day but seldom have to define. We see beauty in a sunset, in a forest, in the architecture of a church, in music, and in a human face. We may not have an exhaustive explanation of beauty, but one of the defining qualities seems to be structure.

For centuries, artists and writers considered structure to be a reflection of the meaningful order of God's creation. "Every aspect of the world was created with a structure, a character, a norm. These underlying principles are God's law—God's design and purpose for creation." [Pearcey, Fickett, and Colson 1999:297] C.S. Lewis said that writers should seek out that design and attempt to find "some reflection of eternal Beauty and Wisdom." [Lewis 1995:6]

Writers don't invent that design or the beauty it reveals. It was here before we arrived and we merely discover it. In his essay on miracles, Lewis touched on this theme: "Nature is being lit up by a light from beyond Nature. Someone is speaking who knows more about her than can be known from inside her." [Lewis 2002:409]

Modern scientists are not inclined to talk about "God's design," yet their observations often bear an uncanny resemblance to the descriptions of theologians and artists. Oxford mathematician Roger Penrose asked, "Is mathematics invention or discovery?" He concluded that mathematicians don't invent truth, but uncover truths that are already there. [Davies 1992:143]

Many of the scientists who laid the groundwork for quantum mechanics and particle physics described their research as a process of following the *beauty* that was revealed through their equations. Physicist Paul Davies writes:

> Time and again, this artistic taste has proved a fruitful guiding principle and led directly to new discoveries, even when it at first sight appears to contradict the observational facts. . . . Central to the physicist's notion of beauty are harmony, simplicity, and symmetry. [Davies 1983:220-1]

Einstein spoke of his admiration for the beauty of order and harmony "which we can grasp humbly and only imperfectly." Paul Dirac said that "it is more important to have beauty in one's equations than to have them fit experiment." David Bohm wrote that "physics is a form of insight and as such it's a form of art." [Davies 1983:221-2]

Richard Feynman said that scientific knowledge "adds to the excitement and mystery and the awe of a flower" [Feynman 1999:2], and he even claimed that physicists "respect the arts more than the sciences." [Feynman 1995:13] Roger Penrose believed that "a beautiful idea has a much greater chance of being a correct idea than an ugly one." [Penrose 1987:421]

These scientists, all of whom worked in the environment that we often refer to as "pure science," were guided by (quoting Paul Davies again) "arcane concepts of elegance in the belief that the universe is intrinsically beautiful." [Davies 1983:221]

It is easy to scoff at writers who seek "beauty" and talk of "God's design." Mathematicians and theoretical physicists who find beauty in their equations make the scoffer's job more difficult.

A structured story reveals beauty and also affirms meaning and purpose in human experience. In doing this, story structure becomes both the medium and the message, the repository of value. "What makes a work of art good as a work of art is its form. . . . In the hands of a great artist, form is intimately related to meaning." [Veith 1991:42 and 44]

Meaning is revealed through the framed events inside the story, a tiny structured slice of experience where we explore the difference between good and evil, right and wrong, sanity and insanity, babble and poetry, order and chaos, courage and cowardice, civilized behavior and barbarism.

On an unconscious level, a structured story teaches that how we live our lives *does* matter and that the decisions we make do have consequences. As Foster-Harris put it, writers "furnish parables confirming the moralities taught by the clergy." [Foster-Harris 1967:22-3]

The mere presence of story structure makes an important statement about moral order—that it exists—and the presence of moral order permits us to seek *justice.* A well-crafted story should leave the reader satisfied that the internal accounting has balanced and that justice has been done. *The characters should get what they deserve.* Tragedy or comedy, a story should resolve into justice.

In a world that is awash in sin and evil, it is sometimes hard to find justice, and the movie *Fiddler on the Roof* provides an example of that. At the end of the story, Tevye and his fellow Jews in the Russian village of Anatevka fall victim to a vicious pogrom and are forced to leave their homes. Their lives are shattered. Where is justice?

When the movie ends, our hearts belong to Tevye and his people.

74

We admire their simple honesty, their sense of humor, their piety, their courage, and the beauty of their traditions, qualities of character that have remained intact. We know they will take their Torah scroll to another land and start their lives all over again.

Their response to evil doesn't destroy evil, but evil doesn't destroy them either. The experience leaves them stronger—and it leaves us stronger too. This beautiful movie makes a powerful statement about the triumph of goodness in the face of evil, and we can be sure that nobody will ever make a beautiful movie about the Russian constable who led the pogrom.

We've all read novels and watched movies that didn't find justice. What do we say about them? I would say *they're bad stories*. They might succeed as history, journalism, or sociology, but they fail as stories. The subject material was too big for the skills of the writer. The story-frame couldn't hold the events inside.

Every subject isn't worth writing about and everyone who scribbles words on a page isn't gifted enough to transform words into a structured story.

A plumber must run a sewer line downhill, a carpenter must build a sturdy house, and writers must find justice in their stories   Structure grows around justice, like iron filings forming geometric patterns around the invisible force fields of a magnet. If we have no expectations of justice, there is no force that will tug events into a structured story.

In the Western world, our concept of justice has blossomed into an elegant system of law that describes how citizens and governments should behave, but justice is not merely a legal concept. How could it be? Justice demands that we make distinctions between right and wrong behavior. Those are decisions of moral judgment that rest on something more substantial than the whim of a single individual or 51 percent of the voting public.

Our Western notion of justice owes something to the Babylonians, Greeks, and Romans, but the laws of the Jewish Decalogue from the hand of the Creator brought something new to human experience: the verifiable communication of divinely given law. Kugel notes that this created a unique legal system. "Elsewhere, to violate the law was a crime; in Israel it was also, explicitly, a sin." [Kugel 2007:683] C.S. Lewis spoke of justice as "the continual hope of the Hebrews for judgment, the hope that some day, somehow, wrongs will be righted." [Lewis 1967:165]

Christians inherited this unique concept and added to it, giving us four thousand years of wisdom and guidance that form the context in which the craft of storytelling operates. Story structure should affirm the truth and wisdom of that tradition. Remove storytelling from its transcendent source of justice—the God who gave us the Ten Commandments and created the universe described by theoretical physicists—and story structure has no foundation. It is a house built upon sand.

This is a matter of concern on two levels. On a strictly professional or business level, the absence of structure in writing destroys our ability to function as storytellers. The story-frame disintegrates. A story cannot exist in a moral vacuum. Tension and conflict, which give a story its sense of movement, require two poles. If there are no poles, there is no tension, conflict, or movement, and no hope of a just resolution.

Stories become banal, empty, and devoid of meaning. Without a reference point, they have nothing to teach, no wisdom to reveal, no justice to affirm. This amounts to a failure of craftsmanship. The storyteller has violated the trust of his audience and delivered a product that doesn't function, the equivalent of a house that falls down.

The second level of concern is something we might call "Author's Liability." When a shoddy house falls down and maims the people inside, poor workmanship escalates into a moral and legal issue. The contractor can be sued.

Can a bad story damage the customer, and should writers bear any responsibility for the damage they cause? I think so, and we'll look at that in the next chapter.

I've talked about the importance of beauty and justice in storytelling, but said nothing about the qualities that have been most apparent in my Hank the Cowdog stories: fun, joy, laughter, and nonsense. Physicist Richard Feynman often described scientific inquiry in whimsical terms, as fun and play, a quest for "the beauty and wonder of the world." [Feynman 1999:185] Dr. Feynman recognized that physics is serious business, but he saw no reason for making it painful to his students.

I have followed a similar approach in my writing. When I take an analytical view of the structure in my Hank stories (something I don't do very often), I see that they actually contain two kinds of movement. The first is the one we've been discussing, the *trajectory* of the story, but there's another—a kind of circular motion that occurs inside the forward trajectory. We find the same two kinds of motion in a tornado: One is forward, the other circular. Both types of motion are part of the same system, but they have different functions.

In a Hank story, the spinning action is where we find much of the comedy: Hank and Drover carrying on loony conversations or Hank going off on one of his long rambles that doesn't always make sense.

In the sixth Hank adventure, *Let Sleeping Dogs Lie,* Hank is racing back to ranch headquarters to bark the alarm about some impending crisis, but on the way, he scares up a cottontail rabbit. He can't pass up a chance to chase a rabbit and off he goes. But then he's drilled by a flea and has to abandon the rabbit to scratch the flea.

By the time he has whacked the flea, he has forgotten the crisis that caused him to run back to the house in the first place. This little digression stopped the story . . . but nobody cares because we had fun laughing at Hank.

I'm not sure where I acquired the model for this type of story structure, but it might have come from watching the films of Laurel and Hardy, Charlie Chaplin, and the Marx Brothers. Those masters of comedy understood that a story should have a beginning, middle, and end, but what you do along the way might be just as important.

Nobody goes to a movie or buys a book to brood over its structure. As writers, we want to affirm moral and aesthetic principles, but if we don't do it in an entertaining manner, we might end up talking to ourselves.

CHAPTER ELEVEN

ART VERSUS CRAFT

"Professing themselves to be wise, they became fools." - Romans 1:22

I remember reading an article written by a well-known author, in which he declared, "I am indifferent to structure in a novel." This was back in the seventies, when just about everyone was rebelling against something, but, still, I thought it astounding that an author would make such a statement.

There is no profession outside the arts that permits a practitioner to invent his craft as he goes along. It happens every day in modern America, where the artistic elite, representing what I call "Uppercase Art," has turned its back on four thousand years of tradecraft and moral tradition. Art today has become what an "Artist" does, and if that happens to be loathsome, too bad.

Francis Schaeffer saw this as a trend that brings together what he called "the new secular mysticism and the new theology." On this view, "there is no certainty that a god is there," and yet "the poet, musician, or art as art is the prophet where there is no certainty about anything." [Schaeffer 1985:75] In a similar way, art as art today appears to have something to communicate, and yet it lacks certainty regarding the means and meaning of art.

The flaw in this mystical and indifferent system is that instead of getting a Shakespeare, who really was a genius, we get a Norman Mailer, who really wasn't. After Mailer spent the early years of his career writing about himself, making himself into a character and then a sad caricature,

79

we find him hustling a book on punk-killer Gary Gilmore, using the advance money to pay alimony to his five ex-wives.

He was the same literary giant who used his influence to win the release of Jack Henry Abbott from a Utah prison. While serving a long sentence for forgery and murder, Abbott wrote Mailer a number of letters. Mailer thought he detected great literary talent, helped Abbott find a book publisher, and lobbied to get him paroled from prison.

"A few weeks after being released, in June 1981, Mr. Abbott, now a darling in leftist literary circles, stabbed to death a waiter in a Lower East Side restaurant," thus confirming an observation made by Martin Amis, that Mailer had a weakness for "any old killer who has puzzled his way through a few pages of Marx." [McGrath 2007:1 and 30]

Mailer paid *no price* for his part in this murder of a mother's son. Great Artists, it seems, have license to maim and corrupt, but they're never around to wash the blood off the walls. That's a job for lowly cops and ambulance drivers who "aren't smart enough" to get into Proud Harvard, Mailer's alma mater.

It's hard to quantify the damage caused by poor writers and bad stories, but a growing number of Americans sense that the book, movie, and television industries are turning out material that damages the human spirit. How could it be otherwise? When young people are exposed, day after day, to stories that can't distinguish between good and evil, stories that deny the existence of justice and any kind of meaning in human experience, how could it *not* cause deep and lasting damage to the society as a whole?

Clearly, a lot of modern writers don't see this as a problem. They find little or nothing transcendent or worthy in Western civilization and seem to think they owe nothing to the tradition that produced the Ten Commandments, the Sermon on the Mount, the Magna Carta, and the U.S. Constitution. Indeed, the more scorn they can pour upon this moral tradition, the more praise they receive for being Serious Artists.

Uppercase Art in modern America has become a synonym for arrogance, irresponsibility, vulgarity, disrespect, and wild, suicidal self-indulgence. It seems to me that consumers of entertainment products would be much better served if writers started viewing themselves as practitioners of a *craft* and stopped pretending to be a kind of secular clergy that stands above the laws of man and God.

There are several important differences between an artist (the modern version) and a craftsman. A craftsman creates for someone other than himself. If he is a Christian, he might view his craft as a vocation, which means that he sees his life's work as a means of revealing part of God's design. He follows a body of craft-knowledge that relates to function, and if his product collapses, blows up, injures or poisons the customer, the craftsman accepts responsibility for the failure.

So many artists today, on the other hand, create for themselves, invent their own rules regarding structure and function, and accept no responsibility for the final product or any damage it might inflict.

We can't blame artists entirely for the spiritual malaise that hangs over our nation, but art is more than a mere reflection of society. It also shapes society. It teaches and provides examples of what it means to be a whole, civilized human being. It points toward a moral structure that human beings crave and need. As C.S. Lewis wrote, "In reality, moral rules are directions for running the human machine. Every moral rule is there to prevent a breakdown, or a strain, or a friction, in the running of that machine." [Lewis 2001:69]

81

But art that believes in nothing teaches nothing—or at least nothing that should make us hopeful about the future of Western Civilization—and the question becomes, *What are creative people doing to protect Western Civilization, the very sea in which they swim?*

Uppercase Art has spent the past four decades kicking the dog of bourgeois Christian morality but offers nothing to take its place, except the dead-end logic of secular materialism—ugly, formless, shapeless, meaningless blobs of experience. In our time, art has suffered "a tragic loss of sacred beauty" [Ryken 2006:12] and that is cause for great concern.

It is no longer sufficient for writers to announce to a benumbed public that all forms of behavior are acceptable, that sex with anything is okay, or that human beings are fated to be slobs. If the public ever buys those cheap ideas in large quantities, writers will be the first to regret it.

Young writers should be speaking out against stories that are formless, chaotic, selfish, and disgusting. Their mission should be to do what artists deserving of the title have always done: bring light into the world, find order in chaos, and provide nourishment, hope, and meaning to people who need it.

Art that can do that is heroic. Art that can't is a fraud.

CHAPTER TWELVE

CROOKED "ACCOUNTING" IN MOVIES

"Great drama leaves the audience free to choose and doesn't try to manipulate."
- Linda Seger, *Behind the Screen: Hollywood insiders on Faith, Film, and Culture*

At some point in the 1970s or 1980s, filmmakers began making movies that masquerade as entertainment but are actually vehicles for proclaiming a social-political gospel. Sometimes the effort is subtle, sometimes blatant, but it always leaves me with the feeling that I'm being manipulated by people I shouldn't trust.

There are many ways filmmakers can manipulate their material (camera angle, lighting, music, costumes and makeup, different lenses), but since I'm a writer, the one I find most annoying is the use of crooked "accounting" in the screenplay. Story structure has its own internal ethical accounting system. Characters acquire debits and credits as the story moves along, and at the end, everything should balance. If it doesn't, something is wrong. The author has been either careless or dishonest.

Conventional screenwriting theory places a high value on the "story arc," broad changes in a character over the span of the movie. Sometimes scriptwriters try to achieve this by introducing the main character as ignorant, selfish, cruel, and vulgar. By the end of the movie, we're supposed to see resolution and redemption.

In theory, this yields the desired effect (a broad story arc), but the accounting doesn't always come out right. Sometimes the guy is such a slob at the beginning, he needs more than ninety minutes to make moral deposits to cover the checks he's written. Ten minutes into the story, we just don't care what happens. We walk out of the theater or turn off the DVD . . . or wish we had.

Sometimes writers try to fudge the accounting by introducing social issues as a substitute for moral qualities of character. Instead of improving himself by making good decisions, the protagonist "improves" by being "right" on a social issue that happens to be in vogue. If he's against the war in Iraq, it doesn't matter that he cheats on his wife, neglects his children, lies to his friends, and steals from his boss.

Bottom line: He's a jerk and crooked accounting won't mask it.

Feminism has inspired a host of dishonest stories. In their frenzy to bring "strong women" to the screen, writers seem to lose all sense of equilibrium. One common trick is to surround a female lead with male characters who are spineless weenies. That's crooked. Why? Honest accounting says that *women who hang out with weak men are weak*. True strength comes from courage and goodness, not from a comparison to mediocrity.

Another feminist trick is to peddle the illusion that the leading lady can shoot, stab, karate-chop, set off bombs, and kick every male in the crotch, and still remain attractive in the traditional feminine sense (nice hair, perfect makeup, warm smile, loving personality). Strength and skill in self-defense are desirable traits, but future generations will laugh their heads off at this ideologically transparent attempt to juggle the debits and credits of human nature, and will marvel that movie audiences ever paid their money to watch such flummery.

Another form of literary embezzlement occurs in films about so-called animals. I say "so-called" because the "animals" in film bear little resemblance to creatures in their natural state. I'm not talking about the classic Disney movies, or the cartoons featuring Bugs Bunny, Tom and Jerry, or Woody Woodpecker. Most of those films were innocent, funny, and charming, and nobody cared that the animal characters had been per-fumed in an animation studio—the most conspicuous example being Walt Disney's mouse.

Realism didn't become an issue until moviemakers began filming live-action animals and giving them scripted lines that carried a social/metaphysical agenda. This blurring of realism, ideology, and fantasy takes the movie into a zone that goes beyond entertainment. Animal movies can be a stealth vehicle for secular preachers because the audience doesn't go to the theater expecting indoctrination.

When dogs, cats, horses, goats, mice, and pigs start preaching, the viewer has a right to demand an audit. Who are these "animals," what are they doing, and why should we listen to them?

In the Hollywood Gospel, animals are portrayed as better than they really are, while the human characters are portrayed as worse. In such films, people kill, eat, plunder, and pollute, while animals are repositories of Wisdom and Goodness. Humans, especially blue-eyed adult males, beat our furry friends, eat them, generally mistreat them, and never under-stand what Life is all about.

For all their warmth and cuddliness, animal movies often seem to be written by people who don't like people very much, and who are grop-ing toward a quasi-religious vision in which animals save the world.

The most admirable character in *Babe* was a vegetarian pig whose story brought home the message that, deep down, pigs are nicer than people. *Because of Winn-Dixie* gave us a dog character that functioned as a four-legged Gabriel on a mission to help the human characters work out their problems. (*E.T.* offered a variation on this theme, with a little visitor from outer space who taught humanity crucial lessons about life in the cosmos.)

But the story accounting is rigged in these films, because *the characters are not animals*, even though we're seeing pictures of live-action animals on the screen The pigs are not pigs, the dogs are not dogs, and the horses are not horses. They have all been distorted through a human lens.

People who live around pigs every day know that pigs are not vegetarians. They will eat snakes, rabbits, the eggs of quail and wild turkey, their own babies, and you, if they get a chance.* People who live around pigs every day don't ask them for advice. People who share their lives with dogs know that if dogs were in charge, the world would be an endless comedy or a complete wreck, probably both. (See the Hank the Cowdog books for confirmation.)

Horses? I own five of them and use them regularly as tools on my ranch. If I can catch them, impose a saddle and bridle upon them, and spur them into doing work, they perform with courage and intelligence. But they don't care about my marriage or how the kids are doing. If I dropped dead in the saddle, they wouldn't feel one shred of grief. They might even celebrate. Without me around, they would be free to pursue the fondest dream of every horse: to do nothing but eat.

---

*This news came from a fellow with long experience in the swine business. He told of a farmer who had been having some heart problems. On his way to feed the pigs one morning, he fainted in the pen. By the time someone found him, he had lost a lot of weight. My informant's sad comment was, "Never assume that a pig loves you."

One is tempted to ask filmmakers, "If you know so little about animals, why are you making movies about them?" They might claim to "love" animals, but their love is a cloistered emotion that doesn't have the smell of the fire. They make the animals whatever they want them to be. *Milo and Otis* gives us scene after scene of animals doing what human filmmakers think they would do if they were dogs, cats, foxes, raccoons, bunnies, and ducks, living in a flimsy world where the characters don't have to reveal how they might respond if they ever got hungry.

On a rational level, nobody believes that animals are celestial beings, but the visual medium is not rationally focused and its messages are subtle, often manipulative, especially when filmgoers suspend disbelief in the search for entertainment.

So we file out of the theater, thinking, "Gee, if we were more like dogs and pigs, this world would be a better place!" When we say that out loud, it sounds funny, but it's not funny at all. It's a reckless message to be planting in the minds of children because it misdescribes what animals really are. It ignores their capacity for stupidity and cruelty, even as it cuts against the very heart of who we are and where we came from, as described in book of Genesis.

Filmmakers might think they can improve on God's design, but since they haven't created anything more substantial than a collection of staged images, we have every reason to be wary.

The dishonest depiction of animals reveals a deep weariness with the human condition, an abhorrence of our sinful nature, and so-called animals provide a temporary, illusory escape from the taint of original sin. If all humans are villains and plunderers, what shall we do about it—become dogs and pigs?

Humans can learn from real animals and appreciate them for what they are, but we don't need a kind of Gospel "revelation" from a synthetic version of them, because we already have a "script" that addresses animal nature and human nature. We have a whole book of verifiable, time-tested wisdom and revelation. It tells us that hogs and dogs and humans are all part of God's creation, but we're not the same.

Humans are made in God's image, which is why we're supposed to take care of animals, instead of hoping they will take care of us.

To be fair, we should note that Christian filmmakers have their own ways of cooking the books. When their stories rush past the Fall in a wild sprint toward the finish line of Redemption, we get wooden characters and shallow plots—propaganda instead of metaphor, preaching instead of story craft. We get a Christian flop that nobody wants to see a second time.

Tricky accounting never works. When you try to bypass the real world and cheat the system, you get a bad movie every time.

CHAPTER THIRTEEN

HANK AND THEOLOGY

"Only the Maker of galaxies would have thought to give mankind such a marvelous gift as a dog." - John R. Erickson, *present volume*

Every year since 1983 I have done somewhere between fifty and a hundred live performances for audiences in just about every state except those in the Northeast, where the idea of importing cultural material from Texas is still viewed with suspicion.

Most of my performances have been in school settings, sometimes private or Christian schools but usually public. I'm there because, when I perform my stories, it creates an interest in reading, even among students who aren't fond of it. Kids who enjoy my programs rush to the library and dive into the Hank books. After they've read my books, they move on to other authors. I get paid for turning non-readers into readers.

Public education in the U.S. has received a lot of criticism in the past decade, much of it deserved, but I have had the honor of working with teachers who were dedicated to their profession in ways that are almost beyond belief. Consider the challenges they face every day.

Public schools have become a dumping ground for every major sociological problem in modern America: poverty, racial unrest, illegal immigration, welfare, child care, broken families, drugs, illiteracy, pornography and child abuse, and the decline of manners, civility, and standards of decency.

It all flows like a big sewer into public education, and when a teacher walks into the school at seven-thirty in the morning, that's what she faces. While the people of America fund eight hours of school-based "free" daycare, while senators and judges and professors and artists invent new ways of dodging questions of morality and value, the teacher takes a deep breath and walks into the middle of it—in her classroom.

There, she must face the effects of a culture that has lost the wisdom and will to make distinctions between right and wrong, up and down, evil and goodness, pornography and art, and she can't dodge the questions. She stands alone in front of the class . . . and what will she tell these children?

The teachers I know are making a quiet stand against the slick barbarism of popular culture. They teach manners and patriotism and reverence and civilized discipline to children, some of whose parents are "too busy" to do it themselves. For this heroic effort, teachers are often maligned by the press, scolded by pious legislators, threatened by the ever-nasty ACLU, and tortured by the paperwork demands of state and federal bureaucrats.

I don't know why teachers go on, holding back the sea, but I'm convinced that if they ever give up hope and walk off the job, America will simply collapse upon itself and cease to function.

When I figured out what teachers do—what they *really do*—and realized that they saw me as an ally, I came to understand that I had become a part of their struggle to hold back the sea.

Most of those teachers were women, and their maternal instincts told them that their children would be safe with my stories. It was the same instinct that tells a mother that children shouldn't play with snakes. I also noticed that most were Christians. Their objective was not to evangelize, but simply to protect innocent children from literary material that might harm their spirits—*and against which they had no means of self-defense.*

Instinct might have also told them that there is something deeply Christian (and Jewish) about the act of reading. Both Christian and Jew are, and always have been, People of the Book. When God chose to give us His law, He didn't draw pictures. "The tables were *written* on both their sides; on the one side and on the other were they *written*" (Exodus 32:15, emphasis added). God's law was written so that it could be *read.*

When Paul and the other apostles wanted to record the events they had lived and witnessed, they didn't beat on drums or communicate through first-century rap songs. They wrote it down so that it could be *read* by future generations.

In their own quiet way, teachers are making decisions about the culture. The ones I've known understand that a story is ultimately an equation that yields insights into meaning, purpose, value, and justice. These elements in balance are what allow a story to make readers either better or worse.

The teachers and I rarely discussed this in the open, but we didn't need to discuss it. They already knew, and they figured it out long before I did.

And then there was the letter I received from a mother. I'll never forget it. Her daughter had recently died of leukemia. She said that during her daughter's last days, the family gathered in her hospital room and read Hank the Cowdog books aloud. It was something they had done in happier times, and she thanked me for the gift of laughter.

I was dumbfounded. When a mother tells you that she read your book to her dying child, you need to sit down and think about it because you're standing on holy ground. What people do at the approach of death has something to do with religious faith.

But how can there be anything theological in funny stories about a dog? The Bible doesn't even say much about dogs, and when it does, the references are hardly flattering. We see them lapping blood, eating crumbs, devouring Jezebel, and licking the sores on Lazarus. (The ancient Egyptians seem to have been fonder of dogs than the Hebrews).

Nor can we say that humor has been a driving force in our Protestant heritage. Of the seven books of theology sitting on my desk at this moment, none has an index listing for "humor," and my *Strong's Concordance of the Bible* shows roughly three times as many entries for "sorrow" as for "laughter."

C.S. Lewis points out that nowhere in the New Testament are we told that Jesus laughed. But Lewis adds, "It is difficult, in reading the Gospels, not to believe that He smiled." [Lewis 1995:4] In fact, He might have had been smiling when he told the disciples, "Blessed are ye that hunger now: for ye will be satisfied. Blessed are ye who weep now: *for ye shall laugh*" (Luke 6:21, emphasis added).

When detractors in the secular press describe Christians as dry and humorless, (the thin-lipped man and wife in Grant Wood's painting *American Gothic*), maybe there's a reason for it.

Over the years, I've gotten some testy feedback from Christians who weren't always amused by what they found in the Hank books. Back in the nineties, we heard from a pastor in East Texas who was upset that the first book contained a scene where Hank eats silage (fermented corn stalks) and gets tipsy.

I got the idea from friends who grew up on farms where silage was fed to hogs and cattle. They told delightful stories about livestock made drunk by green silage. Other stories told of birds made drunk by eating fermented berries off of trees.

Drunken hogs, dogs, coyotes, cattle, and birds make funny stories, and they are part of the organic experience of every kid who has grown up on a farm or ranch, yet the pastor in East Texas seemed convinced that John Erickson was trying to promote drunkenness among school children.

Some Christians have objected to my character Madame Moonshine, a "witchy little owl" who claims to have magic powers. In *The Further Adventures*, Hank is stricken with a serious malady, "Eye-Crosserosis," caused when he spent too much time staring at the end of his nose. He goes to Madame Moonshine, hoping she can cure him.

Her treatment consists of giving Hank a riddle to solve: "How much wood would a woodpecker chuck if a peckerwood's a checkerboard square?" The question is so complex, Hank has to use algebra to solve it, but at last he comes up with a solution: 5.03. Madame Moonshine is amazed (not really) and proclaims him a genius (he agrees), and his vision returns to normal.

I have never met a witch or wanted to, and until recent years, I didn't suspect that they even existed outside of books by C.S. Lewis and L. Frank Bohm. I have used Madame Moonshine's "magic" as a way of injecting humor into the stories and solving plot problems, yet, to my amazement, some Christians find darkness and paganism in the character.

Witch isn't the only word in my stories that has caused alarm. I once had a long discussion with a father who asked if I could guarantee that the expression "what the heck" didn't appear in my stories. I said no, I couldn't make that guarantee, and added, "I would like to move to your hometown. It must be a wonderful place. You don't have much to worry about." We shared a laugh, but he remained wary and didn't buy any books.

Some customers are offended by Rip and Snort, the coyote brothers, because they entertain themselves by having belching contests, something my peers and I did in junior high school. (We were good at it, and very proud). A few customers have complained that Rip and Snort are actually racist stereotypes of "Native Americans," because they speak a broken, grunted form of English, and Hank describes them as "savages." (How else would a ranch dog describe a coyote?)

When I did Hank performances in Chinle and Winslow, Arizona, at both ends of the Navajo reservation, I never heard this complaint, nor did I hear it when I entertained six thousand school children in Tahlequah, Oklahoma, capitol of the Cherokee Nation. Oddly, the people I was alleged to be offending weren't offended. Perhaps they had a sense of humor.

We also heard from a mother who complained about a "sex scene" in one of the books. She had responded to our ad in *World* magazine and had bought a complete set of fifty Hank books. She sent them back to Maverick Books and we gave her full credit.

When pressed for details about the "sex scene," she pointed to a chapter in *The Halloween Ghost*, where Slim Chance, a bachelor cowboy of thirty-two, prepares supper in his shack for Miss Viola, an old maid of twenty-eight. The problem was that they ate alone in Slim's house, unsupervised!

Several years ago, I got into a heated exchange with a Christian filmmaker who had read a screenplay co-written by me and my son Mark, based on the Hank the Cowdog stories (it has yet to be produced). He took the position that Christian writers should scrutinize every line of their scripts to be certain they teach "life lessons" that reinforce a biblical worldview. He felt that our script fell short in that department.

In principle, I agreed with most of what he said, yet I couldn't escape the feeling that under his rules, humor would suffocate. Finally, I leaned across the table and said, "Jim, this is humor. If nobody laughs, *it's a bad script!*" He stared at me for a long time, puzzled, as though it had never occurred to him that making people laugh was something a Christian writer ought to be doing.

Is there something about humor that makes it unbiblical or un-Christian? Are we so solemn by nature, so dedicated to a ministry of teaching that we can't indulge in an occasional outburst of laughter? I would hate to think so. If we are, then in addition to neglecting a welcome gift from our Creator, we've become the caricatures the secular media believe us to be, and we make ourselves easy targets for parody.

The richest source of parody is a character who has no sense of humor, and all too often, *that's us*. The louder we preach, the more ridiculous we appear to those who don't want to hear anything we have to say, and the moment we mention the Bible, the audience reaches for the "off" button.

In the postmodern world, this is a serious problem for Christian writers. Gene Edward Veith calls it "Christian familiarity." The audience has heard the message so often, "the breathtaking truths of Christianity . . . have become humdrum and mundane," causing the message to "fade from our personal and cultural consciousness." Veith says that C.S. Lewis wrote his *Chronicles of Narnia* in an attempt to "defamiliarize" Christianity. [Veith 2008:30-1]

I would suggest that humor can achieve a similar result and that it does teach "life lessons," but outside the usual didactic method employed in nonfiction writing and documentary storytelling. Didactic teaching involves a fixed relationship between teacher and student: *The teacher always controls the message.*

In humor, the impact of the message is never quite under the author's control. When the audience laughs, we're never sure whose face has caught the pie.

This makes humor a risky medium. Maybe the audience will laugh in the right spots and maybe they won't. Maybe they will view the story as biblical and maybe they won't. Maybe they will grasp the nuances of meaning that humor can expose and maybe they won't. Humor is a gift from author to audience, and once it's passed along, it can't be called back. Writers who insist on controlling the message will never feel comfortable taking such a risk.

A lesson that humor can teach is that when we take ourselves too seriously we are committing the sin of pride. The author of Proverbs knew a lot about pride and had some choice words to say about it. "When pride cometh, then cometh shame (11:2) . . . Pride goeth before destruction, and a haughty spirit before a fall (16:18) . . . A man's pride shall bring him low: but honor shall uphold the humble in spirit (29:23)."

Jesus listed pride as one of the "evil things that come from within and defile the man" (Mark 7:22). C.S. Lewis called pride "the Great Sin . . . the essential vice, the utmost evil . . . the one vice of which no man in the world is free; which every one in the world loathes when he sees it in someone else; and of which hardly any people, except Christians, ever imagine that they are guilty themselves." [Lewis 2001:121]

Excessive pride not only cuts us off from our fellow man, but also from God. Again, C.S. Lewis: "In God you come up against something which is in every respect immeasurably superior to yourself. Unless you know God as that—and therefore, know yourself as nothing in comparison—you do not know God at all. As long as you are proud you cannot know God." [Lewis 2001:124]

Lewis saw humor as an antidote to pride and used it to great effect in his work. In discussing Lewis's approach to humor, Terry Glaspey wrote:

One of the powerful truths about humor is that it assumes an ideal against which we judge ourselves. If there were no ideal or expectation to fall short of, there would be nothing to laugh about . . . Humor helps us to realize that from God's point of view the self-important human being is a pretty funny creature! [Glaspey 2005:128]

Indeed, a Christian worldview should throw a bright light on the humor in our human dilemma—that we are part-angel and part-animal, shaped by Divine Intelligence but built out of mud, and find ourselves sharing this planet with spouses, parents, children, politicians, and preachers who are just as odd as we are.

The possibilities for comedy are endless, yet we Christians have not exactly set the world ablaze with our humor. But humor has always been present in the oral tradition of storytelling where jokes, malapropisms, yarns, riddles, aphorisms, and puns have provided a much-needed source of strength and release. *Reader's Digest* wasn't the first to figure out that laughter is good medicine or that funny stories about dogs speak a universal language.

I have often thought that the bond between humans and dogs shows the unmistakable stamp of Divine Intelligence. Dogs are so perfectly suited to be our companions, it couldn't have occurred by chance.

They're always glad to see us when we come home. They love us when we're unlovable and forgive our every shortcoming. They have learned to fetch our birds, herd our livestock, guard our homes, and baby-sit our children. They teach us humility and make us laugh. When they die, they break our hearts and remind us of our own mortality.

As the saying goes, a dog is our best friend . . . *and that couldn't have been an accident.* The incredible bond between humans and dogs brings the arguments against intelligent design to a dead stop because when you add up all the atoms in a dog and all the atoms in a human being, you don't get the joy and love that have bound us together for unknown centuries.

Only the Maker of galaxies would have thought to give mankind such a marvelous gift as a dog, and my wife has observed many times that dogs are living proof that He has a sense of humor.

Chapter Fourteen

Hank as Parable

"God built a thousand questions, but only two hundred and fifty answers."
- Hank the Cowdog

Although Hank is just a dog, in his character and actions we find parables that remind us of people we've known . . . even ourselves. *The Curse of the Incredible Priceless Corncob* gives us a little parable on wealth that illustrates the message in Psalm 49:16-17: "Do not be over-awed when a man grows rich, when the splendor of his house increases; for he will take nothing with him when he dies."

In this story, Hank thinks he's become a wealthy dog. This comes about one evening when Sally May, the ranch wife, throws out some sup-per scraps that include several corn cobs. At first, Hank is outraged. Corn cobs? He doesn't eat corn cobs and has no interest in them . . . until he notices that the chickens want them.

That changes everything. He drives the chickens away, takes pos-session of the cobs, and spends the next several days guarding them. The longer he guards them, the more the chickens want them, and the more convinced Hank becomes that the cobs are worth a fortune. He talks about it in a song called, "I'm Rich."

Well, sudden wealth can do a lot to change your attitude.
Makes you aware of who you are and what you have to prove.
I mean, you can't just go on living in the same old low-class style.
You've got to put on airs and flaunt your wealth and strut your stuff

a while.

For one thing, it ain't proper now to speak to just anyone.
You've got to choose your friends more carefully, according to how much mon
They've got. 'Cause, see, a lot of dogs don't have it, and probably never will,
And them's the kind you leave behind when you're marching up the hill.

It says YOU'RE RICH!
You're rich.
No more sleeping in the ditch, old pal, this dog is rich!

This episode was inspired by the bizarre behavior of one of our ranch dogs, and it raised the question, "What is wealth?" An object acquires value because someone wants it. We can laugh at a dog that thinks a corn cob is worth a fortune, but then we look around and see humans who are just as infatuated with stock certificates and hundred-dollar bills. Their response to pieces of paper is every bit as silly as a dog barking chickens away from an old corn cob.

The Case of the Tricky Trap illustrates another verse of Scripture, Proverbs 26:11: "As a dog returneth to his vomit, so a fool returneth to his folly."

King Solomon, who "spoke 3,000 proverbs" (1 Kings 4:32), must have owned a dog, and probably observed a ritual that I've seen many times on our ranch. In the spring of the year, when the first sprigs of green grass appear, dogs eat it—why, I don't know, since they are alleged to be carnivores. But they eat grass, often so much that it makes them sick.

100

In *The Tricky Trap*, Hank gorges himself on green grass and even lectures Drover about the importance of adding "salad" to his diet. Later, riding in a warm pickup, he begins to feel sick. When reverse peristalsis takes command of his body (Hank calls it "reverse perestroika"), Slim Chance stops the pickup and throws him out.

The cowboy yells, "Hank, do me a favor. When you throw it up, don't eat it again."

Hank is insulted by the suggestion that he might eat his own vomit, but after tossing up the green grass, he finds himself staring at the puddle on the ground and sees "sprigs of green parsley floating in a French sauce. Hmmmm. You know, some experts claim that parsley is actually good for dogs, and all at once . . . never mind."

"So a fool returneth to his folly." Hank is both a dog and a fool, but his problems go even deeper.

> Hank wants to be a good dog, but he's involved in a constant struggle with his nature: a short attention span, food lust, and an exalted opinion of his role as Head of Ranch Security. He's a *sinner.* Sometimes he rises to heroism but he doesn't stay there for long. That describes every dog I've known. It also has some very funny parallels with the human condition. [Interview with the author by Susan Olasky, *World Magazine,* December 2, 2006, pp. 26-7]

As Head of Ranch Security, Hank is in charge of protecting Sally May's flock of chickens from coyotes and raccoons, but inside his mind, he's dying of chicken lust. He wants to eat them so badly, he can hardly stand it! His doggie soul is thrown into a permanent twist between duty and appetite. In the fifty-first book of the series, *The Case of the Blazing*

Sky, he sings a song that describes his dilemma:

> Chickens, all I see are chickens.
> It really is the dickens
> When the mind plays clever tricks,
> Projecting colored pictures
> Of a bird upon a plate,
> Such a cruel fate.
>
> Dinners, all I see are dinners.
> Just exactly what a sinner
> Doesn't need, it's so frustrating
> To see roasted birds parading
> Down the Broadway of my mind.
> Destiny's unkind.

Every minute of every day, he struggles against the sins of pride, lust, gluttony, sloth, and deceit, and at some point, instead of hearing Hank's narration, we begin hearing the voice of the Apostle Paul, saying, "I do not understand what I do. For what I want to do I do not do, but what I hate, I do" (Romans 7:15 NIV).

When we see spiritual torment in a dog, it's funny. As we watch Hank drift toward temptation, we shake our heads and laugh, knowing exactly what he's going to do and what will come of it. Part of the humor, I suspect, is that we've been there so many times ourselves—*and we know that our sins are a lot worse than bumping off a few chickens.*

In these three examples, we find a dog teaching biblical lessons, but without any mention of the biblical text. Can we say that the Hank stories are Christian? I think they are, but in a subtle, indirect way.

The beauty in the stories arises from a worldview that traces beauty back to its ultimate source, the God of Creation—and you don't have to be a Christian to recognize it. The reader responds to the beauty, structure, truth, and humor, and somehow in the interplay of those elements, something else emerges: spiritual nourishment.

This is a gift that Christian writers can pass along to their readers, even to those who think they don't share our faith.

Chapter Fifteen

Stories as Nourishment

"Good writing, like good food, needs to be savored; it is nutritious."
- Gene Edward Veith, *Reading Between the Lines*

I was surprised the first time an elementary school librarian invited me to read my Hank the Cowdog stories to her students.

I knew nothing about children's literature and never dreamed that children could understand the subtle humor in a story whose main character might be summed up in a paraphrase of St. Paul's lament in Romans 7:15-6: "That which I do, I should not, and that which I should not, I do -- all the time."

Hank, who narrates the stories, exaggerates, often tells little lies to cover his mistakes, has no self-knowledge, and . . . well, isn't very smart. That's pretty subtle, and I wrote the first Hank book for adults, not children.

Seven million-plus books later—most of them purchased by or for children—it's obvious that I wasn't a marketing genius.

I have received many letters from parents and teachers who said, "Thank you for giving our children something decent to read and for allowing them to enjoy innocent laughter." Some letters gave me a jolt. They came from teachers of dyslexic children who had never read a book until they found Hank. Others came from mothers of children afflicted with that mysterious condition known as autism.

After I had gotten three of those letters in the space of a month, I wrote back to one of the mothers and asked, "What is your child finding in my stories? I know nothing about autism."

She pointed out that autistic children fight a constant battle against mental chaos. They crave structure and order. My stories are orderly and structured. They all have twelve chapters and the same cast of characters. They all begin with the same sentence, "It's me again, Hank the Cowdog," and most end with, "Case closed."

They all have happy endings and in every story, justice is affirmed. When Hank makes a dumb mistake, he pays for it. When he makes a good decision, he enjoys a moment of triumph—before he blunders into another mistake.

Those letters didn't come from literary critics. They came from mothers and teachers who were involved every day in the process of nurturing—giving life. And from them I learned that my business is not books. It's nourishment.

I'm not much inclined to give theological interpretations to stories that were meant to be funny, but those letters forced me to think about the spiritual dimension of storytelling.

The opening chapters of Genesis tell us that God's first act of creation was to create an orderly cosmos out of nothing, and then to impose additional structure on that primeval creation, for example, separating the dry land on earth from the water, day from night, earth from sky, and male from female.

As Francis Schaeffer has pointed out in *Genesis in Space and Time*, this creative activity reaches back ultimately to the character, goodness, and personality of the Creator Himself. And it makes possible structure and life in a moral universe where distinctions between right and wrong, just and injustice, have real meaning. Without a divinely given structure, there is no adequate explanation or basis for making distinctions between these opposites. All we have is chaos. [Schaeffer 1972:13-66]

A structured story says, without saying it, that there is order in the universe, and in this crazy postmodern world, that becomes a profoundly positive religious statement, an affirmation of the divine act of creation. Kids are drawn to it by instinct because they have a natural craving for structure and meaning. We all do.

And yet popular culture offers just the opposite: frantic television images that have no coherence, movies that can't distinguish between heroes and villains, art that seems to have lost all vision of form and beauty, books with characters we would never invite into our homes, and jagged "music" that offers neither a melody nor harmony.

If the word *art* has any meaning, then surely it should aspire to something higher than the disorder that any fool can perceive on so many street corners in any American city on any given day. If artists are more gifted than the rest of us (we keep hearing that they are), then let them find the order and harmony that are not so obvious to ordinary mortals.

Let artists return to the ancient notion that art and literature should nourish the human spirit, not poison it.

That statement would draw chirps of laughter in most college English departments, where the health of the reader seldom receives any consideration. If readers are spiritually maimed by their exposure to literature . . . well, too bad. You can sue a plumber who does shoddy work but not an author who gives his readers toxic waste packaged between the covers of a book.

The enumeration of chaos in art, literature, and music strikes me as a particularly loathsome form of obscenity. If Marshall McLuhan was correct in saying that the medium is the message, then the message in chaotic art forms is that we live in darkness on a planet that God has abandoned.

And you don't have to look far to see the results. In August 2004, I was honored to be a featured speaker at a Texas Home School Coalition convention in Houston. On the trip back to the Panhandle, my wife and I notice the startling contrast between the young people we saw in the airports and those we'd met at the convention.

The homeschooled children at the convention were serene, clear-eyed, polite, clean, at peace. They seemed to know who they were, and their sense of identity began in the knowledge that they are part of God's creation. From that everything else flowed naturally. Their home-based education was a process of learning about the roles we are meant to play in a plan that was here before we were born, a plan we don't have to re-invent every day.

In the airports we saw many children of pop culture: young people with empty eyes and graceless gestures; girls who showed no hint of modesty or virtue, and boys, flabby and tattooed, staring at nothing and bobbing their heads in time to the clattering sounds piped into their brains through headphones.

Their appearance suggested a generation whose only purpose is to consume and feel good, and then, like summer moths, to die. Their faces revealed the tragedy of lives without structure, including the wonder of God's plan. (It seems odd, though, that they don't fly in unstructured airplanes and probably don't want the pilots to be undisciplined ninnies.)

What we choose to see, hear, and read matters greatly. People need good stories just as they need home-cooked meals, clean water, spiritual peace, and love. A good story is part of that process. It affirms divine order in the universe and justice in human affairs—*and it makes people better than they were before they read it.*

Wouldn't it be nice if writers used that as a standard for measuring their work? It makes more sense than fog-bound theories that allow them to peddle rubbish under the name of "literature."

I find sad irony in the fact that, while mothers of dyslexic and autistic children fight day and night against mental chaos, popular culture pumps it out by the ton, infecting young people who were blessed with normal bodies and brains and leaving them twisted and adrift.

If writers can't improve the lives of their customers, then what is the purpose of literature? Surely there is more to art than impulse, fame, and paychecks.

CHAPTER SIXTEEN

THE CHRISTIAN WRITER

"Christian art is redemptive, and this is its highest purpose."
- Philip Ryken, *Art for God's Sake*

Let us return to St. Paul's "Great Commission" to artists and writers: "Finally, brothers, whatever is true, whatever is noble, whatever is right, whatever is pure, whatever is lovely, whatever is admirable—if anything is excellent or praiseworthy—think about such things . . . and put [them] into practice" (Philippians 4:8 NIV).

Yes, that covers it pretty well. "Although this verse has wider implications for the whole Christian life," notes Philip Graham Ryken, "at the very least it outlines a set of ethical and aesthetic norms for the artist and for art." [Ryken 2006:44] When a story resolves the conflict and drama of the plot, we want the reader to think on the things that are true, honest, just, pure, lovely, virtuous, and worthy of praise.

But we should notice that the qualities listed by St. Paul are the *finished products* of a Christian life. He speaks as a man who has already been redeemed, and in his role as preacher, he is saying, "This is where you want to be at the end of your spiritual journey."

Preachers can *tell* us that, but storytellers must *show it.* You can't begin a story with the ending. You can't start a story with the finished product. You can't reach a resolution without tension and conflict. To put it into Christian terms, you can't have redemption without the Fall, or resurrection without the crucifixion. It's bad theology and it's worse storytelling, because it departs from the basic template of story structure: a

109

story begins, moves, and resolves.

If we view St. Paul's life as a three-act screenplay, his letter to the Philippians would fall near the end of Act Three. To get the rest of his story, we must go back to Act One. There, we see a very gifted, literate, articulate Hellenized Jew named Saul. In Act Two, we find him watching as Stephen is stoned to death, and using his talents to "breathe out threatenings and slaughter against the disciples of the Lord" (Acts 9:1).

Then he is blinded on the road to Damascus and hears the voice of Christ: "Saul, Saul, why persecutest thou me?" (Acts 9:4) His life is changed and resolves into Act Three, where he offers sound advice in a letter to the Philippian church.

A lot of Christian writers (me included) don't like Act Two because that's where we find an emphasis on fallen man and all the nastiness of the broken human soul: cruelty, adultery, and violence, the temptations, bad choices, and stupid mistakes. We know where we want to be and where we feel most comfortable (Act Three), and we're prone to rush through the second act, covering our ears and holding our noses.

There, safe on the other side, we *tell* the audience to think on the things that are true, honest, just, pure, lovely, virtuous, and worthy of praise. And it doesn't work. We get a story that is sentimental and dull, with characters who speak in soft tones and smile all the time.

We get a "good Christian story" that *isn't a good story.*

Dr. Thom Parham, an associate professor of theater, film and television at Azusa Pacific University, and a Christian, has written a blistering critique of movies made by Christian filmmakers. He lists fifteen films made between 1995 and 2004 and says, "Overall, these films are unwatchable. There are only a handful of good scenes among them. None had success with critics or at the box office. . . . Most films that successfully incorporate religious themes are made by nonreligious people."

Christian filmmakers, he says, are so intent on their message, they ignore storytelling and production values. Further, they "tend to see the world the way they want it to be. Ignoring life's complexities, they paint a simplistic, unrealistic portrait of the world. . . As long as people of faith are more concerned with messages than metaphors, they are doomed to make bad films." [Lewerenz and Nicolosi 2005:54-8]

Independent filmmaker Isaac Botkin agrees. "With few exceptions, films made by Christians are a frustrating mixture of ideological conformity and poor production quality." [Botkin 2007:97]

When novelists and screenwriters stop telling stories and "go to preachin'," Christian literature shrinks down to one book, and we surrender our national culture to people who don't read it. We need both preachers and storytellers, but not in the same time and place. If we have any hope of influencing popular culture, our stories must compete in a secular marketplace and *win,* and that means we have to master story craft and produce better stories than the competition.

That won't be an easy assignment. In the environment of modern popular culture—or "postmodern," as some observers have described it [Veith 1994; Pearcey 2004:242-4]—Christian writers operate at a disadvantage. We don't feel comfortable in Act Two, yet Act Two is where popular culture lives and thrives.

That's where we find all the noise and action: loud parties, cheap sex, hard drinking, gruesome murders, bombs exploding, politicians cheating on their wives, athletes who fail as role models, television preachers

111

who fleece their followers and bed their secretaries, and Hollywood stars who are proud to announce that they've produced babies out of wedlock.

Popular culture *loves* Act Two! It's a fool's paradise, populated by adolescents of all ages, who are dedicated to their own pleasure and believe they will never die. This is the sphere of life that yields the gaudiest movies with retina-blasting special effects, the soapiest soap operas, and the most riveting hours of evening news, "all designed to bypass the mind and appeal directly to the senses and emotions." [Pearcey, Fickett, Colson 1999:467]. And, unfortunately, this is where authors these days can make the most money writing books and screenplays.

But secular writers have story-structural problems of their own. If Christian storytellers are hobbled by a tendency to look past Act Two, non-Christian writers have trouble *getting out* of Act Two. Their stories can't find true resolution or redemption. The chords begun in Act One and Act Two never resolve, and Act Three becomes a hollow celebration of "our humanness."

Lonesome Dove and *The Thorn Birds* might serve as examples. Both were lavish, entertaining, and successful TV dramas that ended with the death of a main character, Gus McCall in *Lonesome Dove* and Father Ralph in *The Thorn Birds*. Death brought down the curtain, but the stories never resolved. They merely stopped.

Of the two problems (our stories lack tension and drama, their stories can't find redemption), ours may be the easier to remedy, because our Book gives us plenty of material that deals with Act Two, if we will take notice. The Act Two material begins in the third chapter of Genesis, and goes through the entire Old Testament and into the New.

We have mentioned the dramatic story of the Apostle Paul, but we

112

find an even better example in the life of Christ. Every year at Easter, we relive the historical drama of an innocent man who was set up by politicians, betrayed by a friend, tried in a kangaroo court, abandoned by his comrades, tortured, mocked, and murdered in front of his own mother.

His last words, "It is finished" (John 19:30) seem to be a statement of total humiliation and defeat, yet the whole point of the story is that *it resolves in victory*. "Christ is risen, alleluia!" That is the message at the end of the Easter service when the organ blasts out the postlude and the congregation places flowers on the bare wooden cross at the front of the church.

If Christian writers have become squeamish about Act Two, we need to look closer at our own roots. Our message begins with the wonder of life in the garden, but then moves to betrayal and murder. The liturgy of the Easter season is not for sissies, as Mel Gibson made abundantly clear in his movie, *The Passion of the Christ*.

But how do we show the fallen world without becoming a part of it? How do we deal with explicit sex and violence, and language that is brutal, vulgar, and blasphemous?

Some Christian writers would argue that art, even Christian art, must describe "reality as it is," warts and all. But I wonder, what is so "real" about violent language and explicit sex? The fact is, most of what we call literature *did not* swim in those waters, and most of the great storytellers who ever lived never dreamed of taking the kind of liberties that modern writers seem to think is their birthright. We could fill an entire book with the names of authors who didn't.

Until a few decades ago, writers worked within the constraints of public taste as defined by the Judeo-Christian tradition. Even more radical (to modern ears), writers considered themselves *part of the community that created those constraints*. Did it limit their freedom of expression? Of course it did, but every craft imposes limits. Plumbers aren't allowed to run sewer lines uphill. Roofers can't invent new ways of laying down shingles. Diamond cutters are not free to express their whims in the shape of a gem.

In most professions, freedom is limited by some concept of public good and that seems to be a missing element in a lot of modern writing. Does the open display of sex and violence *improve* the average citizen? If our books and movies teach first-graders to speak the language of thugs and half-wits (the ever-quotable C.S. Lewis called them "trousered apes"), will the community be better for it?

Centuries of Christian tradition say no. Popular culture doesn't seem to care or even ask the question.

Today's college students might be surprised that families of my generation used to attend movies on a regular basis, two or three times a week, and objectionable content was simply not an issue. Granted, some of those movies were sappy and sentimental, but others would have to rank among the best ever made. *One-Eyed Jacks, On the Waterfront, High Noon, Casablanca, The African Queen, Singing in the Rain, Gone With the Wind, The Miracle Worker,* and the Wallace Beery/Jackie Cooper version of *Treasure Island* come to mind.

I own all of those movies on VCR or DVD and have watched them many times. I study them and never fail to learn something every time I view them. I had watched *Casablanca* three or four times before it occurred to me that Rick and Ilsa were carrying on a sexual affair. Their romance was handled with such a light touch that you could see it as sexual or not, and it didn't affect the story either way.

114

In *Treasure Island* Jim Hawkins befriends the pirate Long John Silver. As the story progresses, we begin to understand that Silver is a *bad* man. In a casual manner, he mentions that he murdered thirteen of his comrades in their sleep, using a hammer as his weapon. Silver reveals himself as a fallen man, but he does it without uttering a single expletive, and we don't have to watch him bludgeon all thirteen of his victims. The screenwriter was kind enough to leave something to the imagination.

But what about a movie such as *Schindler's List*? It was a very ambitious film that attempted to capture the magnitude of the Nazi atrocities during World War II. It included scenes of appalling violence—and I don't want to watch it again. The inclusion of graphic violence diminished the aesthetic value of the film and detracted from the story. The subject overwhelmed Stephen Spielberg's attempts to describe it in a framed work of art. In my view, *Schindler's List* might have succeeded as a documentary but not as a story.

Some subjects simply cannot be approached in a direct manner. If we wish to view an eclipse of the sun, we must use indirect methods, either watching it through a shadow box or protecting our eyes with smoked glass (the kind welders use). Otherwise, the brilliance of the sun will cause permanent damage to the eye. When God appeared to Moses in the burning bush, "Moses hid his face, because he was afraid to look at God." [Exodus 3:6 NIV]

Perhaps the same principle applies to the kind of unfathomable evil that engulfed Nazi Germany. If we try to describe the horror in a direct manner, our stories fall apart under the stress.

A story is not the same as a documentary. Nor does it give us the kind of experience we would get from a security camera at the local museum: a stream of unedited facts. A story can't tell us everything about a subject, and the artistry comes in what we *don't* show.

One of the best movies I've seen on the Holocaust was a quiet little film made by Hallmark, *Miss Rose White*. It showed the impact of the Holocaust on one Jewish family living in Brooklyn. It had no war scenes, no blood, no brutal language, yet it was very effective in conveying the emotional impact of an unspeakable tragedy on the lives of five people—not through documentary scenes of brutality, but through great storytelling and great acting. That is artistry.

When I hear novelists and filmmakers declare that they're only describing the "world as it is," I keep wondering, "Are they doing this for me or for themselves?" As a viewer and consumer of cultural products, I can't escape the feeling that the vivid depiction of violence, sex, and brutality deadens part of my soul. It cheapens me and it cheapens the artist because, as Gene Edward Veith has pointed out, obscenity is more than a moral failure; it is an artistic failure as well. [Veith 1990:36].

And that includes the use of brutal language. What is the magic in gutter language? It has only been in the last thirty years that novelists and screenwriters have turned the F-word into an all-purpose noun, verb, adjective, and adverb. How did Homer, Virgil, Dante, and Shakespeare manage to record the human drama without it? How did poor mortals express their feelings of extreme anger and joy?

They did it with skill and imagination. They did it with language that was rich in texture, tone, and nuance.

There is no great magic in that word or any other expletive. In fact, their use is a symptom of intellectual sloth. Any writer who depends upon one expletive (or even three) to express the full range of human emotions is no better than a composer who uses one finger to peck out a tiresome little melody on the piano.

Could the makers of *The Godfather* and *The Shawshank Redemption*, both excellent films, have told their stories without scatological language? Of course they could have! There is not one crime or emotion in those movies that hasn't been recorded in the Old Testament, *The Iliad, The Brothers Karamazov,* or Shakespeare's plays—without language that was corrosive, degrading, or offensive.

Such language serves the writer, not the audience. It's an adolescent indulgence that allows rebellious scribblers to stick a thumb into the eye of Christian (or Jewish or even Muslim) propriety.

My personal view is that Christian writers can show the complexity of human experience without abusive language, explicit violence, or Peeping-Tom sex. I don't accept that "reality" must be bloody, bawdy, or blasphemous, lurid, lewd, rude, shocking, or ugly. Those qualities might describe a *slice* of reality, but hardly all of it. My library shelves are crammed with books by authors who walked through the second act of the human drama with their eyes wide open. They saw man in his fallen state but didn't wallow in it.

How much of the fallen world do we have to show? Marvin Olasky has suggested this interpretation of Philippians 4:8: "We should meditate on God's excellencies and praise Him—and we should think about those even more lovingly in juxtaposition to the sin around us. In short, the heavens show the glory of God, the streets display the sinfulness of man, and we learn from both." [Olasky 2008:50]

We must show enough of the fallen world to establish tension and conflict in our characters, enough to make redemption more than an abstract idea, and enough to create stories that are honest and beautiful. We can achieve that by viewing human experience through a Christian world-view, though we may have to build our own infrastructure (publishing companies, websites, film companies, and distributors) to get our stories to the people who need them.

Francis Schaeffer, Nancy Pearcey, Gene Edward Veith, Jr., Marvin Olasky, C.S. Lewis, Josh McDowell, and others have told us that the Christian worldview offers a broad, comprehensive, coherent vision of human experience on this earth: where we came from, why we're here, and what we're supposed to be doing. The Christian worldview reveals "truth about the whole of reality" [Pearcey 2004:16] and offers a sensibility "that is so vast and comprehensive that it embraces the intellect and the heart, accounting for both objective truth and subjective experience." [Veith 2008:62]

Surely this gives us an advantage in seeking the truth that expresses itself in beauty. Secular humanism can't explain where beauty comes from or why observers from fifteen different nations, all speaking different languages, can gaze at the same flower and perceive that it's beautiful.

The Christian worldview offers a simple explanation: Beauty is one of the Creator's gifts to mankind, and we are hard-wired to recognize it. "Christians, unlike the secular culture, have a basis for affirming the personal and the beautiful—a personal God who created structures of beauty in the very texture of the universe. Christians, therefore, ought to cultivate what is aesthetically worthy." [Veith 1991:37]

We see the beauty of creation as it appears in shapes, forms, colors, relationships, and, yes, even in humor. Secular materialistic art sees only the random movement of electrons with man at the center—man who has appetites but no hope, purpose, or meaning. Uppercase Artists might argue that they're describing some kind of objective truth, but what they're seeing isn't objective at all.

They are seeing what their limited worldview allows them to see. Blindfolded, they're feeling the elephant's tail and calling it an elephant.

In *How Should We Then Live?* Schaeffer talks about the British/ French Concorde airliner. It was designed by engineers in the sixties, a time when "intellectualized art" was rebelling against order, form, structure, and traditional notions of beauty, yet many observers described the design of the Concorde as beautiful, even a work of art.

When asked about this, Sir Archibald Russel, the British designer, replied, "When one designs an airplane, he must stay as close as possible to the laws of nature . . . . It so happens that our ideas of beauty are those of nature. Every shape and curve of the Concorde is arranged so it will conform with the natural flow as conditioned by the laws of nature." [Schaeffer 1976:196]

If an Uppercase Artist designed an airplane, he would make it ugly and dysfunctional. He would design it to *crash,* not to fly, because crashing would satisfy his death-wish for the human race. But engineers, following mathematics and common sense, created a device that not only would fly, but also captured the beauty inherent within the laws of physics—the same beauty that was described by Einstein, Bohm, Feynman, and Dirac.

What Sir Archibald called the "laws of nature," we would call God's design, and it would not be stretching things to say that the aesthetic qualities we recognize in the Concorde bear a strong resemblance to those mentioned by St. Paul in Philippians 4:8, confirming that "aesthetic principles, no less than scientific principles, are grounded in the created order and are a manifestation of God's design." [Veith 1990:48]

The qualities Paul listed in the text from Philippians 4 (true, honest, just, pure, lovely, virtuous, and worthy of praise) are not exclusively Christian concepts, for they arise from God and are available to all of humanity via creation in the image of God. In Paul's day, they were understood by speakers of Greek, Latin, Hebrew, and Aramaic; by Greeks, Romans, Jews, Africans, Asians, Egyptians, and Southern Europeans. Today, those words have been translated into more than two thousand languages. They are universal concepts and can be understood by Christians and non-Christians alike.

Ultimately, Christian authors should measure their work against a set of aesthetic principles that apply to all writing. We don't have a separate Christian category for Beauty, just as we don't have a Christian Law of Gravity. When we aspire only to "Christian art," we run the risk of aiming too low and limiting our audience. Our audience should be the same one Paul was going after: *the world*. And it can be, if our art seeks the beauty that is so apparent in God's creation.

Writers sell their wares in a marketplace of ideas and entertainment, and it's a *huge* market. We compete for consumer dollars and for bookstore shelf space against the best authors who ever lived—not just the best writers of the present day, not just the writers who call themselves Christians, but also Hemingway, Dickens, Tolstoy, Dante, Shakespeare, St. Augustine, and the unknown author of *The Epic of Gilgamesh*, written five thousand years ago in what is now Iraq.

We are even competing against St. Paul himself. Among his other gifts, Paul was an extremely successful writer whose books, the Pauline Epistles, have remained bestsellers for almost two thousand years.

The spiritual nourishment that arises from beautiful art is universal in its appeal. Though it might begin as "Christian art," it has the potential of reverberating far beyond the confines of a church sanctuary. If that work is noble, true, right, just, pure, excellent, beautiful, and praiseworthy, it will be perceived as such in Chinese as well as in English, on Time's Square as well as in the First Baptist Church in my hometown.

The human spirit responds to beauty because God designed us to find nourishment in beauty. The goal of Christian writing should be to discover the beauty expressed in symmetry, structure, and coherence, and then to do a professional job of describing it in stories that are shaped by the most influential book ever written.

If we describe it well, non-Christian readers will see that it's beautiful. At some point, maybe they'll ask where it came from . . . and we can tell them.

- PART THREE -

THE TOP 20 -- IF I WERE TEACHING A CLASS ON WRITING

CHAPTER SEVENTEEN

8 KEYS TO GOOD WRITING

"The answer to bad books is good books."
- Gene Edward Veith, *Reading Between the Lines*

I have never been employed as a teacher or had to face the task of teaching a class on writing, and I give thanks for that. I might enjoy teaching for a week, but after that I would find it tiresome to hear myself talking for hours every day.

Also, I would be operating under a handicap because I'm not convinced that writing can be taught at all, and, if it can be, I'm not sure that a classroom would be the best place to do it. My own experience has caused me to think that only a few of us are meant to become writers, artists, and musicians—and most are not. Those with that destiny often know it at an early age, can't explain where it came from, and can't be stopped. The others can't be pushed, coaxed, or led into a vocation that wasn't meant for them.

Further, I'm aware that my approach to writing has been highly subjective and rather eccentric. Consider that:

- The teacher who influenced my writing the most never went to college or wrote anything longer than a letter.
- Even though I read every day, I don't consider myself well-read on any subject.
- My approach to writing owes at least as much to oral-tradition storytellers as to the written tradition of European and American literature.

- I spent years reading novels and studying fiction techniques, but haven't read any fiction since I published the second Hank the Cowdog book in 1983. Okay, one novel, written by my pastor.
- I learned very little in the writing courses I took in college.
- I served my literary apprenticeship writing for livestock publications, not for *The Paris Review* or *Atlantic Monthly.*
- I have received rejection slips from every major publishing house in the United States, and from many of the smaller ones too.
- After fifteen years of failure as a writer, I had to self-publish the first ten Hank the Cowdog books.
- My original audience for the Hank books was 100% adult. I knew nothing about children's literature and still don't, yet I am known as an author of children's books.
- My books have never appeared on anyone's Best Seller list, Christian or secular.
- I seem unable to write about anything but my experience as a cowboy and rancher.
- I don't watch television.
- I know very few authors and rarely attend literary functions.
- Kris and I live on a ranch, forty miles from town, and I spend more time with dogs, horses, and cattle than with people.
- I follow a daily routine that I compare to a mule pulling a plow.

This should confirm that my approach to writing has been odd, and my opinions on writing are only opinions. They were chiseled out of the hard rock of experience, but another writer might regard them as complete nonsense.

Every time I hear composer Eric Satie's "Gymnopedie Number 1," I am reminded that skilled artists are able to find beauty in places I have never been or even dreamed of. I can't imagine where he found his haunting melody and harmonies, but I'm grateful that he wrote the piece. I think it's beautiful—and nothing in my experience can tell me why.

But let us suppose that something about writing can be taught, that I have a few insights that are worth passing along, and that you have some curiosity about hearing them. Read on in this and the next two chapters for what we might call Twenty Principles from the Hank the Cowdog School of Writing.

1. The first ingredient in good writing is content, not style.

If you've taken a writing course or read a few books on writing, you've probably run into the word "style." I did, and I never figured out what it meant. I always suspected that everyone but me knew about style.

It took me a lot of years, and a lot of manuscripts that went to the city dump, to figure out that style is what remains after the writer has finished the job. It appears at the end of the process, not at the beginning, like the vapor trail that follows a high-flying jet aircraft.

It's not something we should try to cultivate, in other words. Our job as writers is to reveal content, not to establish style. If the content is good, the style will take care of itself. If the content is dull or dishonest, no amount of style will conceal it.

In a good story, the individual words blend together and become invisible. Readers lose the sense that they are reading, as though the story were reading itself or were being told by an unseen narrator. The reader is aware of the story, not the style.

One result of this is that we might not even recognize our best writing until someone points it out. This has happened to me several times and it always came as a shock.

In 1981, I wrote a series of humor articles for *The Cattleman* magazine, twelve articles that drew on my day-to-day experiences as a ranch cowboy. I wrote them strictly for money and without any thought about their literary value, and turned them out at a rapid clip, one article per day for two weeks.

In 1982, I read some of those stories aloud to the Rotary Club in Perryton. Rotarians are always looking for a speaker at their weekly lunch meetings and I was looking for an opportunity to let people in my community know that I was trying to be an author.

One of the stories I read was "Confessions of a Cowdog," a short story that featured two dogs I had met on ranches, Hank and Drover. I didn't think it was anything special or even the best in the series, so I was astounded by the response it got from the Rotarians. They howled with laughter and after the program, one of them came up and said, "John, you need to do more with that dog!"

Up until that day, I had never suspected that there might be magic in those characters. Shortly thereafter, I started writing the first Hank book. It scares me to think that if I hadn't done that thirty-minute program for the Perryton Rotary Club, I might never have developed the Hank series.

Here's another example. On a hot, windy Sunday in March 2006, a fire broke out on the 6666 ranch in Hutchinson County, Texas, and went roaring across the northern Texas Panhandle. It was an enormous fire that burned, off and on, for five days, killed twelve people, and scorched close to a million acres of ranch land. Our ranch on the north side of the Canadian River was right on the edge of the fire, and for most of a week, we lived in fear that a shift of wind would send it our way.

On the third or fourth day of the fire, I decided that I needed to write down my thoughts and observations, so I wrote a long letter to my friend, author John Graves of Glen Rose, Texas. It was just a letter, not a piece of "writing," and it contained no "style," just facts and feelings.

A week later, I received Mr. Graves' reply. "This is excellent and you should get it published." The thought of getting it published had not occurred to me, but on Mr. Graves' suggestion, I sent it to Jesse Mullins, editor of *American Cowboy* magazine. He sent back an immediate response. He bought the story and ran it in the September issue.

Unknown to me, he also entered the story in the National Cowboy Museum and Heritage Center's Wrangler Awards contest . . . and it won. Best magazine article of 2006.

Both the Hank story and the fire story had strong content and were written without any literary ambition of creating a "style." I wrote them quickly and without much effort. The effort came before the writing—living the events and knowing the characters. The writing itself was just a matter of capturing the details in simple declarative sentences.

2. Good writing communicates information and emotions to someone besides the writer.

At one time in my life, I worked with bricklayers and carpenters. I always admired their ability to build a good honest structure and then walk away from it. They didn't sign their names to it and it never occurred to them to think, "This is my house, my brick wall." When they had done their best job, they left and gave it over to someone else.

We writers have big egos, and sometimes it's hard for us to remember that our purpose is not to build monuments to ourselves, but rather to communicate. Yes, our names go on manuscripts and we want to get paid for our work, but we write for someone else. We are translators and interpreters of experience. We should always be aware of the audience, speak to the audience, and respect the audience. If we speak only to ourselves, we have failed to communicate.

What makes our writing good is not just that we did it, and put our best effort into it, but that someone else benefited from it.

3. *A good story is composed of good paragraphs that are composed of good sentences.*

Let's return to the example of the bricklayer. When he lays up a wall, he goes through a ritual that is simple and even monotonous: mortar, brick, measure, level, mortar, brick, measure, level. When he's finished, there stands a brick wall that is plumb, level, square, and sturdy.

The magic a bricklayer brings to his work is his constant attention to fundamentals and small details. Every brick must be set in the proper way. Every batch of mortar must be mixed right. It's simple . . . if you can do it.

It's the same with writing. The bricks in our craft are words, and the walls we build are stories.

When I was a young writer, I wasn't content to build good honest walls. I wanted to build cathedrals. Instead of using plain brick, I tried to use granite blocks. Instead of describing the specific, I wanted to go straight to the universal. But even a cathedral is built one stone at a time, and if you can't lay a simple course of bricks that is plumb and level, you shouldn't be in the cathedral business.

I had to learn to lay brick and spread mortar, which in our craft means learning to use nouns and verbs. "Jesus wept" is a simple declarative sentence that contains powerful emotional content. The power doesn't derive from the words themselves, but from the subject.

These two simple words convey action and emotion and an element of suspense—why did he weep? It's a good sentence and, as odd as it might sound, I would hold it up as an example of good writing. There is no "style" here, nothing flashy, no fancy words from the thesaurus. It just does the job a sentence is supposed to do. It communicates information and emotion. It contains solid brick and good mortar.

Put enough of those sentences together and you might have a good story.

4. Good writing is clear, not obscure.

It should be obvious that good writing is clear, yet there is so much obscure prose in our society, it makes you think that someone doesn't believe in clarity.

Every day we come into contact with obscure writing: owners' manuals for chainsaws, tractors, cell phones, pickups, and electronic gadgets; "serious" literature, contracts, insurance forms, government reports, and all communications from the IRS.

When I was in college, I sometimes got the feeling that our professors cultivated techniques for writing opaque prose. Their objective was not to communicate or to clarify, but to use language as a tool for intimidating the reader, to make the reader think, "Well, if I can't understand what he's saying, he must be a lot smarter than I am."

It is the writer's job to communicate. If he doesn't, it's his fault, not the reader's. Clear writing originates in clear thinking, and clear thinking finds its natural expression in lucid prose.

At this point, you might accuse me of having a bias against complex forms of writing, some of which might appeal to readers whose minds are more scientific, philosophical, or poetic than mine, and I have to agree. My opinions about writing are highly subjective and should be weighed against the opinions of others.

I admire simplicity. Some writers don't, and I would rather not put myself in the position of saying that Hegel, Marx, Bergson, Hume, Kant, Tillich, Melville, Joyce, and others, who caused my eyelids to sag, were bad writers.

C.S. Lewis is a writer for whom I have acquired an enormous admiration, but I found his essays hard to penetrate at first. I started and quit *Mere Christianity* three times before I was finally able to finish it. Sometimes I had the feeling that I was peering through a microscope and watching as Lewis pulled tiny hairs with tweezers and wove them into a delicate tapestry. In reading his essay on miracles, I often felt that he had disappeared into a fog that stretched for entire pages. I could still hear him, but had no idea what he was talking about.

Under my rules, Lewis did his best writing in *A Grief Observed*. There, still stunned by the loss of his wife, Joy, he spoke in a voice that

132

had none of the embellishments of a poet, none of the complexity of a theologian. The voice was stark and bare, like a man muttering aloud. Listen:

> "I look up at the night sky. Is anything more certain than that in all those vast times and spaces, if I were allowed to search them, I should nowhere find her face, her voice, her touch? She died. She is dead. Is the word so difficult to learn?" [Lewis 2002:662]

This is English prose that goes straight to the bone. I don't think that Lewis ever wrote better prose than in that essay on grief. But you know what? I'm thankful that he wrote exactly as he wrote and didn't ask my opinion. His phenomenal success as a writer speaks for itself.

5. *Good writing is active, not passive.*

Compare these two sentences. First, "Jesus wept." Then, "Jesus was observed weeping." Which is the better sentence? Number one, "Jesus wept." It is direct, honest, and clear.

Sentence number two speaks in the passive voice, and notice what has happened. We have doubled the word count, but have we doubled the information or emotional impact? No. In fact, we have diminished the integrity of the statement by injecting a question that is never answered: Jesus was observed weeping . . . *by whom*? Who did the observing?

The best way to analyze a sentence is to diagram it: subject, verb, object. A diagrammed sentence imposes discipline on the author, forcing him to see the parts of speech and how they relate to each other. It sharpens the focus and tells us exactly who did what to whom. (If I taught a writing class, I would encourage students to diagram their sentences.)

Out of clarity comes honesty. Diagram a sentence in the passive voice and you expose its lack of honesty. One of the most often-used statements in modern politics and diplomacy is, "Mistakes were made." If you diagram that sentence, you find that the subject is "mistakes," but it is *receiving* the action instead of causing it. Hence, we have a semantic cover-up for some unknown skunk who made the mistakes.

The sentence is actually saying, "Okay, we have a real mess here, but we're not going to tell you who did it." If "mistakes" are the villains, nobody gets fired and nobody can be held accountable. But when you put the sentence into the active voice, you know where to put the blame: "I made mistakes." Subject, verb, object. We have clarity and honesty.

The passive voice encourages fuzzy thinking and even shady behavior. That's why people who are under indictment, dodging responsibility, or have something to hide often choose the passive voice. It's the natural mode of expression for people who don't want to be identified or understood.

6. Good writing consists of good sentences made of nouns and verbs.

Let's go back to our example of "Jesus wept" and jazz it up a little more, not only casting it in the passive voice but throwing in an adjective and an adverb: "A distraught Jesus was observed weeping sorrowfully."

Here, instead of the original two words, we have seven. We have increased the word count 350% and have gained . . . What? We have added nothing but words and noise. If Jesus wept, we don't need to add that he was distraught or that he wept sorrowfully, because intelligent readers can figure it out.

When we add words, we don't always add meaning. Old Solomon made this point when he said, "The more words you speak, the less they mean." [Ecclesiastes 6:11, *Living Bible*] We should use adjectives as spice, not meat, and regard adverbs as something close to poison.

As a young writer, I thought that adverbs created emotion: happily, sorrowfully, mournfully, wistfully, and so forth. Those are words that ought to create emotion in the reader, right? But they don't. The emotion in a piece of writing originates in a mysterious way. If the author feels emotion, those feelings will reach the reader through nouns and verbs and, in fiction, through characters. If the emotion is genuine, the author doesn't have to pump it up with adverbs.

When I see a lot of adverbs on a page, it tells me that the author doesn't feel what he's trying to write and is trying desperately to convince me that he does. I don't like adverbs. There is just something counterfeit about them and most of the time, they insult the intelligence of the reader.

Did you notice that I used an adverb in the previous paragraph? *Desperately.* I used it to give you the thrill of catching me, and also to acknowledge, however grudgingly (there's another one), that adverbs have a place in our kit of tools. But we must use them with care. (I almost said "carefully.")

7. Good writing deals with the specific instead of the general.

Look at this statement: "Back during the Second World War, times were pretty tough."

135

That is the sort of comment people are apt to make when they look back on their lives. Maybe it means something to the speaker, but it doesn't tell the rest of us very much about life in those days. There is nothing specific that the reader can grab onto. You'll notice that the subject of the sentence is "times." Times is an abstract concept, not a person. Times don't do or feel anything.

Now look at this statement:

"During the war, my husband was on a ship in the Pacific and I never knew from one day to the next if he would come home. My youngest child had never seen his father and the other two cried at night and asked, 'Where is my daddy?'"

That little vignette contains specific details and strong emotions. It doesn't tell us everything about the war, but it gives us some insight into what the war meant to my mother and her three children. Given this information, the reader can draw broader conclusions—not only that times were hard but that average citizens made sacrifices and performed acts of heroism on a daily basis.

We reveal the universal through the specific. A war is too big to comprehend, but we can catch a glimpse of it in the story of one family.

8. What is the proper writing "voice"?

Several years ago, I corresponded by email with a friend. He wrote good letters and I told him so, and one day he sent me an article he had written. I usually don't read outside manuscripts, but he was a friend and asked for my honest opinion, so I gave it.

The article contained a number of sentences written in the passive voice. The subjects of those sentences were not people but abstract concepts. I told him that it created a fog that concealed the human characters and their emotions, including his own as the narrator.

I sent him a sample text that contained what I considered good writing: one of his own letters.

It often happens that when we try to write something "important," such as a novel, story, or poem, we become self-conscious. We try to be profound and authorial. We concentrate on the elegance of individual sentences and forget that all writing is a communication between one person to another—a process we follow in a letter without even thinking about it.

My friend accepted the critique of his article and admitted that he had tried to keep himself out of the story. He didn't want to write about himself. That was a noble instinct, but somebody has to drive the bus.

Formal writing, especially fiction, offers a writer the opportunity to conceal his identity and to wear disguises. That can be fun and beneficial, but at some point the reader deserves to know who's doing the talking. And, turning it around, the narrator should have some idea to whom he's speaking.

Those are the two main questions involved in choosing a writing voice: Who's telling the story and who's listening?

Good writers don't always write good novels and stories, but they usually write good letters. In a letter, the whole process is reduced to its simplest level. We know who is talking and who is listening. We have established the identity of the narrator and have defined the audience.

For that reason, it is often a good idea for a beginning writer to compose the first draft of an article or story as a letter to someone he knows and trusts. It makes everything simple. You can always go back and make changes in a later draft, or leave it in letter form. St. Paul wrote some of those and they are still being read two thousand years later.

The narrator in your story doesn't have to be "me," your actual physical self, but that's the most natural place to begin. I am the character I know best. Start simple and build from there. Learn to skate before you play hockey. Before you try to build a house, learn to measure a board and make a square cut with a saw.

CHAPTER EIGHTEEN

8 TRAITS OF GOOD WRITERS

"The best way to drive out a bad worldview is by offering a good one, and Christians need to move beyond criticizing culture to creating culture."
- Nancy Pearcey, *Total Truth*

9. Aspiring writers should be producers, not consumers.

We could list several reasons why aspiring writers, especially Christians, should limit their use of television, but for our purposes, we can trim the argument down to one main point: Watching television is a passive experience that turns the viewer into a consumer rather than a producer.

Anyone who claims to have ambitions of becoming a writer can't afford the luxury of being a heavy consumer of entertainment.

Television is only one of many time-wasters. Modern society offers us a host of others: email, the internet, video games, iPods, movies, cellular phones, amusement parks, sporting events, and beer gardens.

Our society is a consumer's paradise, but when you're consuming, you're not producing. A writer must produce.

10. Writers learn to write by writing.

At the University of Texas, I had a friend who once told me, "I'm thinking of going to Mexico to do some writing." I didn't know much about the writing profession back then, but I found myself wondering what kind of special magic he would find in Mexico. If he wanted to write, why couldn't he do it in Austin?

My friend was what we might call a "professional non-writer." I haven't seen him since the sixties, but I would bet that if he went to Mexico, he read a few novels and wrote exactly as much as he'd written in Austin. Nothing. If you met him at a social gathering today, he'd probably tell you that he's still thinking of going to Mexico to do some writing.

When I encounter people who say they want to become writers, I ask, "Are you writing now?" If the answer is no, I don't have much to say. Writers don't talk about writing or read about it or dream about it or take courses. They do it.

Talkers talk. Dreamers dream. Writers write.

To write, you don't need a college degree, a license from the state, a financial statement, a credit report, a foundation grant, or a note from your mother. You don't need a laptop computer, an office, or even a desk.

All you need is a pencil and a pad of paper. Oh, and it helps if you have something to say.

11. A writer should have something to say.

I once did a program at a homeschool convention. After the program, I sat at a booth and signed books. A twelve-year-old boy came striding up and tried to give me a manuscript. (I declined the offer.) He announced, "I've written a novel and I want you to help me get it published." His father walked up just then, beaming with pride.

Clearly, I was in the presence of a young genius. Early achievement and fatherly pride are worthy of praise, but the realist in me wanted to say, "So you've written a novel at the age of twelve. That's pretty amazing. In your twelve years on this earth, what have you done that is worth a reader's time and money? What stories do you have to tell?"

That's what I wanted to say but didn't. The last thing a young novelist wants to hear is that he might not be a genius.

Content is the most important ingredient in good writing. "Content" means "something to say, a story that needs to be told." At the age of twelve, Mozart was writing operas, but most of us don't have great music or great stories inside us at such a tender age. Sometimes it takes decades for those stories to take shape. Sometimes they don't come at all.

You can teach students to compose sentences that are solid and honest, but how do you teach them to put *life* into their words? Where do we find stories?

I found story material working as a ranch cowboy. Louis L'Amour worked as a prize fighter, lumberjack, and hunting guide. Mark Twain drove steamboats on the Mississippi River and panned for gold in California. Alexander Solzhenitsyn spent a decade in the Soviet gulag. Dostoyevsky served time in a czarist prison. Arthur Conan Doyle worked as a ship's doctor, and made long voyages to Africa and the Arctic. Herman Wouk served in the U.S. Navy during World War II.

But we don't always have to visit exotic locations to find stories. Novelist Elmer Kelton spent his youth on an isolated ranch in West Texas, and later worked as an agricultural journalist. Poet Baxter Black started out as a large-animal veterinarian, as did Ben K. Green. Many writers have discovered characters and stories through their work as teachers, lawyers, doctors, nurses, social workers, or ministers. Erma Bombeck found delightful stories in a place where most people would never think of looking, in the daily experiences of a suburban housewife and mother.

Oftentimes, story material is right in front of us, and all we have to do is open our eyes and notice it—at weddings and funerals; in a church, airport, supermarket, or hospital room; at a rodeo or family reunion. The common thread in all these examples is that we're not sitting around watching television or playing video games. We're not merely describing the wallpaper in our bedroom or the pattern of our brainwaves.

Before we write, we should *live*.

Somewhere in this big world, there may be a twelve-year old who has stories worth telling, but most of us need to spend some time accumulating experience, and maybe wisdom too, from some sort of activity outside of ourselves: building a house, punching cows, baking bread, comforting a sick child, burying loved ones, raising a garden, laughing at dogs, gazing at the stars, keeping a marriage strong.

The easy part of writing is the writing. The hard part is finding something to say that is worth a reader's time.

12. Good writers revise and polish.

Our English teachers were right about this. Your first draft might be pretty good, but it doesn't reach perfection until you revise and polish. Young writers don't want to hear that, but it's true.

We can use the present volume as an example. I wrote the first draft in two months, but spent the next year and a half revising: adding, subtracting, polishing, refining, simplifying, clarifying. I would guess that I made at least fifty passes through the text, and I continued the process right up to the last possible moment.

The chapter on structure was the most difficult piece of writing I've ever attempted because it required a kind of non-fiction thought process that isn't my usual mode. I had to describe the intuitive process of writing humorous novels, using the language of a theologian or a scientist. I can't even guess how many times I read and re-read those pages, but with every revision, it got tighter, sharper, clearer, and better—I hope.

Most of my Hank the Cowdog books sit for three years before they appear in print. During that time, I might go back and do twenty revisions. After the first couple of passes, I'm not making structural changes, but rather small revisions that enhance the rhythm and texture of the sentences.

"Rhythm" is not an easy concept to explain. I don't know that every writer has a sense of rhythm in language, but I certainly do, perhaps because I so often read my stories aloud. When an editor changes my text, I know it immediately. I can feel it and most of the time, it doesn't feel right. The editor might have changed the text for legitimate reasons, but, to me, it alters the flow of the words and makes them less musical.

The "texture" of a piece of writing is easier to describe, and we can find an analogy in a piece of furniture, such as a table. When you run your hand over the surface of a well-made table, you don't encounter snags, splinters, or bumps. The surface has been sanded and buffed so many times, it is perfectly smooth. That is the kind of texture I hope to achieve in a story. The language has been polished to such a high gloss that the

143

reader's mind never hits a snag.

Another analogy would be a water slide at an amusement park. Once you enter the slide at the top, you go flying all the way to the bottom. In a story, your mind flies over the words and, before you know it, you've reached the last page. I suspect that texture is important to me because I've always been a slow reader. I look for ways of making the reading process as pleasant as possible.

The first draft of a story is the equivalent of a table that has been assembled. The wood has been measured and cut, the screws installed, the joints fitted, the legs leveled. The structure is sound and functional. You could eat on the table at this point, but you could also get splinters in your hands and elbows.

13. Good writers read but don't neglect experience.

Writers are often avid readers and are prone to gather story material from books rather than from first-hand experience. Sometimes that works well (it didn't turn out badly for Margaret Mitchell, who never served a minute in the Confederate Army, or for C.S. Lewis, a professor and voracious reader), but sometimes it produces a kind of infinite regress, like images in a hall of mirrors: books that reflect other books and writers who reflect the insights of other writers.

Back in the seventies, when I was experimenting with different types of writing, I spent a whole year writing a thousand-page novel about the Comanche and Kiowa Indians and their struggles against the encroachment of Anglo settlers in the 1870s. To accomplish that, I had to acquire a small library of sources on that period.

I thought the novel was brilliant (naturally), until I attended a writers' convention and met five other authors who had written the same kind of novel, using the same twenty books that had made me an expert on frontier history.

All at once it struck me that none of us had any first-hand experience with the subject, were writing about something we really didn't know, and were dressing up our ignorance with someone else's research.

I don't know what happened to those other novels, but mine still sits in a box in my office, and I'm pretty sure that's where it belongs. Reading can expand our horizons and deepen our knowledge of the universe, but we shouldn't neglect hands-on experience as a source of story material.

14. Good writers use the subconscious mind.

When I was young, my father sometimes talked about solving problems in his sleep, and he was a firm believer in "sleeping" on a major decision. I didn't pay much attention to this and saw no evidence of it in my own life, until I was grown and trying to make a living as a writer.

Somewhere around the age of forty, I began to notice. I would take an unresolved problem to bed and wake up in the middle of the night with a strong conviction that I should take a certain action. The action itself wasn't always new or surprising. Often, it had been one of several options I had thought about during the day, but somehow my sleeping mind had ended the debate and rendered a clear verdict.

I have made some important business decisions in this manner, including my decision in 1990 to buy a 6,000 acre ranch that we really couldn't afford. For weeks, I wrestled with the numbers, my mood making wild swings from sheer joy to sheer terror. Then I woke up in the night with one clear thought: This opportunity would never come along again in my lifetime, and we *had* to figure out a way to buy the place.

We did, and paid it off twelve years later. It remains one of the best decisions I've ever made.

My subconscious mind has also helped me write songs and solve plot problems in my novels and screenplays, and these insights seem to come out of nowhere. Sometimes I get out of bed and write them down, and sometimes I don't. I can't say they've all been useful, but most of them have been.

Ordinary life is loaded with miraculous events, if we pause long enough to notice them. It's a miracle that we can walk across the room, coordinating the movement of billions of cells, nerves, and muscle fibers. It's a miracle that anyone can play the piano, type a letter, fall in love, and survive the assault of a common cold, and we can add "night-time writing" to the list.

I am struck with wonder that a portion of my mind, over which I seem to have no control, is working in my behalf when the rest of me has shut down for the night.

I don't understand the subconscious mind—where it resides, how it functions, or why it chooses to bless my life instead of causing mischief. I'm content to view it as yet another breathtaking marvel in God's creation, and I'm glad to use it in my vocation as a crafter of stories.

I suspect that most of us have this. . . whatever we call it: gift, talent, skill, or blessing, and it can be very useful for people who are involved in creative professions. When "someone" is working nights to help you write good stories, and not asking for overtime pay, it's a pretty sweet deal.

How do we cultivate the subconscious mind? I can only suggest that it might help to live by the Ten Commandments, go to bed with a clear conscience, get adequate sleep, and pay attention to those insights that come in the middle of the night.

15. Good writers are disciplined: Perspiration vs. Inspiration.

When I do programs in schools, I usually leave some time for kids to ask questions. They are curious about where my Hank the Cowdog stories came from, and almost without fail, they will ask the question in the same manner: "What *inspired* you to write the Hank stories?"

It amuses me that they think of writing in terms of *inspiration*. I wrote my first Hank story as an article for *The Cattleman* magazine and my "inspiration" was money, sixty-five bucks, that I needed to support a wife and two small children.

A plumber doesn't wait for inspiration to lay a water line. A surgeon doesn't have to be inspired to remove an appendix, and a professional writer doesn't sit around waiting for the muse to whisper in his ear. He has to make his own inspiration, and that happens when he follows a pattern of disciplined work.

When I'm asked how long I've been writing, I say that I began in 1967, the year Kris and I joined our lives together in marriage. Before Kris, I wrote when I had an idea or felt inspired. After Kris, I wrote every day—same time, same place, a pattern I still follow forty-two years later.

This morning, I rose at five o'clock, joined my dog Tango at the front door, and walked 400 yards to my little writing office. It was black dark, so I had to use a flashlight. On reaching the office, I turned on the lights, started coffee brewing, and turned on my laptop computer. When the coffee was ready, I poured myself a cup, and started working on this project, while Tango chased moths out on the screened porch.

I don't know if I was inspired or not. I didn't stop to think about it. I began writing because that is what I do every morning at this time. The routine takes the place of inspiration.

16. Good writers know that every story isn't worth writing.

Young writers have to figure out what they should write about. What is a proper subject? Out of all the characters we meet in an average week, which ones will make good characters in good stories? Many writers, even Christian writers, would say that any portion of human experience can be a proper subject for a novel or screenplay. I don't agree.

When I first began tinkering with the idea of being a writer, it never occurred to me that I could or should write about my own background. On Mother's side, I came from a long line of cowboys, ranchers, and pioneers in West Texas, and grew up in a small farming and ranching community in the Texas Panhandle. I was pretty sure that rural West Texas had never produced anything worth writing about, so after high school, I left town with no intention of ever going back.

I headed for the big lights of New York City and later spent two years in Cambridge, Massachusetts. For years, I tried to write novels that dealt with city people, city life, and city problems. Naturally, I thought my novels were brilliant (I was one of those little geniuses) but they weren't. They were dark, depressing, and false, and I'm thankful that none was ever published.

Some people can write well about life in the city, but I wasn't one of them. I loved New York City, with all its noise and soot and shoving crowds, its rainbow of cultures, and the hubris of its architecture. But I wasn't able to turn that material into stories that had structure and coherence. What I experienced in cities wasn't worth writing about, and it's too bad that it took me so long to figure it out.

I made another error that grew out of a comment I heard in a college writing class. One of my fellow students, who seemed pretty sharp, said, "If you want to study human nature, you need to work as a bartender."

I did that. For three years, back in Texas, I poured shots and observed human nature in a noisy laboratory fogged with cigarette smoke. I studied the employees and customers and made brief notes on cocktail napkins. Later, I wrote them up as character sketches. After three years, I had filled two ring-binder notebooks with typed notes . . . and to this day, thirty-five years later, I have never used one word from those sketches.

Why? Because in a cocktail lounge, you never see human nature at its best. When people are being served in a setting of leisure, they tend to become self-absorbed, demanding, ungrateful, loud, shallow, vulgar, and overbearing. Liquor makes them worse, transforming good citizens into noisy caricatures who chatter and have little to say.

If you want to study human nature, go where people *work*, not where they play. The part of human nature that is revealed in a bar is exactly the part we want to hide when we're sober, and should. It's mostly shallow and depressing, and I found that it wasn't worth writing about.

A lot of human experience isn't worth writing about, and that is an important insight. Everything we do is not worth repeating, and every human activity doesn't lend itself to the discipline of story structure. A story is not merely a videotape of human encounters. A story, properly done, imposes structure on human experience and gives it a shape that reveals order, justice, and value.

CHAPTER NINETEEN

4 STRATEGIES FOR SUCCESS

"Writers are often tempted to sell out their art in a bid for commercial success. As a result, they try to appeal to the lowest pleasures of a mass market, offering nothing more than time-killing titillation."
- Gene Edward Veith, *Reading Between the Lines*

17. Writers don't need a psychiatrist for writer's block.

Several years ago, I was astonished to read that in cities such as New York and Los Angeles, psychiatrists have set up practice to serve a very specific type of patient: writers who are suffering from "writer's block." To treat it, the practitioners use psychotherapy and even prescribe medication.

Writer's block is something I've read about but have never experienced myself. As I understand it, there are times when professional writers enter into periods when they lose their creative impulses and have nothing to say. If they happen to be under contract to a book publisher, a television studio, or a national magazine, it becomes a problem.

When I say that I've never experienced writer's block, that doesn't mean that I've never gone through dark times when I had nothing to say and began to wonder if I had come to a dead end as an author. I've gone through a lot of those bad times and some of them lasted for months. But I always came through them and didn't need a psychiatrist or a prescription to do it.

I don't like the term *writer's block,* especially the implication that it's some kind of pathological condition, as though writers should be "unblocked" all the time, and if they're not, they need psychotherapy and drugs. It strikes me as wholly unnatural and out of synch with God's design.

What others call writer's block I would call a fallow period or a time of restoration. When we eat a big meal, we lose our appetite. If we have day, we must expect that night will follow. We love the glory of spring, but we can't avoid the groan and bite of winter.

That's not pathology, *it's the way things are supposed to be.* We can't have ice-cream-cones-forever. Unlimited sex, donuts, happiness, or creativity are simply not options for human beings. It's something even Americans shouldn't expect.

I have no advice for New York writers who are under contract and have to produce a book, but I will offer a few words to writers who are just starting out.

Don't believe in writer's block. Don't go to a psychiatrist. And most of all, don't contaminate your body chemistry with whatever kind of potions they're prescribing.

Night must follow day, winter must follow summer, sleep must follow activity, and there will come a time when you don't have anything to say. When that comes, you will have to wait.

While you wait, write in your journal. Tell your journal how much you hate being a writer. Write letters to all your friends and kinfolks. Tell them how you wish God had called you to be a plumber, not a writer.

152

Write character sketches, but not in a bar.

Study the Bible. Chop firewood. Listen to Bach or John Rutter or Gregorian chant. Play an instrument. Read a Hank the Cowdog book. Do something that pulls your mind away from yourself.

We should remember what Terry Glaspey learned from C.S. Lewis:

In *The Screwtape Letters,* C.S. Lewis reminds us that we will experience seasons of great spiritual awareness as well as seasons of dryness and emotional desolation. These he calls 'peaks' and 'troughs.' We should rejoice in the 'peak' times but not lose heart when we find ourselves in the 'troughs.' The troughs are a part of the normal cycle of our spiritual lives, not a punishment or abandonment by God. [Glaspey 2005:155]

Surely the darkness will pass. If it doesn't, if you still don't have anything to say, then maybe you've said it all and you're not supposed to be a writer. It won't be the end of the world. Most of the people on this planet aren't writers and they seem to be doing all right.

18. How do I get my book published?

This is a question I often hear from aspiring authors, but I have placed it here, far down the list of topics, for the obvious reason that if you haven't written a book, you don't need to worry about getting it published.

Writing a book isn't an easy task. Writing a *good* book is even harder. When you've accomplished that, you might think you're home free and the world will be waiting to embrace you as a journeyman author.

153

That's not likely to happen. You might be the only author you've ever met, but there are a lot of us. In the United States alone, publishers turn out something like a hundred thousand new books every year. To put it mildly, the competition for readers and bookstore space is ferocious. When you consider that you're competing for a limited number of consumer dollars, against other entertainment media—cable television, movies, newspapers, magazines, the internet, video games—the picture grows even darker.

So there's the bad news. Writing a book is only the first of many obstacles you will face as an author. Getting it published is likely to be an ordeal, a long process that can be very discouraging. The world's response to your masterpiece could very well be, "Go away, we don't need another book!"

At that point, you either give up or keep plugging along. If you decide not to quit, congratulations . . . and prepare yourself for some difficult times.

A lot of people pass their manuscript around to friends and kinfolks, and try to get some outside opinions. I did. It's a natural first step and a good thing to do, but you have to keep something in mind. *Their opinions really don't matter.* The only opinions that matter are those of the people in a publishing company that will put up money to publish your book. Those are the people you have to please and convince, and if you succeed, they might offer you a contract. Your friends and kinfolks won't do that.

I always encourage beginning writers to study a reference book called *Writers' Market.* It is updated every year and you will want to get the most recent edition. It lists most magazine and book publishers in the U.S. and devotes several paragraphs to a description of what kinds of material they might be looking for. It also has a section on how to prepare a manuscript and how to write a proper query letter. Always send a query letter. Never send the manuscript.

Most public libraries will have a copy of *Writer's Market*, but if you're serious about being an author, you should buy your own copy. Read it from cover to cover, mark it up, and write notes in the margins.

I have heard of writers who found a publisher right away, but for most of us, it's a long process that can stretch into years. While you wait, don't quit your day job (see below). If the publisher offers you a contract, it's a good idea to run it past an attorney, preferably one who specializes in entertainment law. And that applies even if you're dealing with a Christian publisher.

It will cost you some money, but it's a good investment. The main purpose of a contract is to state in simple terms the nature of the professional relationship: who does what, who gets what, and for what period of time? The contract should anticipate problems that we think will never arise but often do. Lawyers are trained to look for worst-case scenarios.

First-time authors don't have a lot of leverage in negotiating a contract, but you don't want to sign a legal document that makes outrageous demands. Some contracts shouldn't be signed. (See my chapter on Disney.)

What about those publishing companies that advertise in magazines and say they're looking for unpublished writers? If all else fails, if you can't find a conventional publisher to do your book, if you're desperate to see your book between hard covers, it might be something to consider.

But be aware that they won't pay the bills. *You* will, and it will cost you in the thousands of dollars. You might end up with a nice-looking book, which they will deliver to your garage, and then you have to go out and sell it. That is where the battle is won or lost because "vanity publishers" don't offer much help in sales. You have to find readers who need your book and are willing to shell out the money and buy it.

19. If you want to become a professional writer, have a skill that will support you.

Writing is a very tough, competitive business, and every writer I've known went through years of lean times. Even if you're a brilliant writer, it might take the world a decade to figure it out. In the meantime, you'll need a day-job to pay the bills.

You have to protect yourself from being crushed by failure, but also from being seduced by "success." Let's say that you sell three or four books to a major publisher and are living well on your advance money. You buy a house and a new car, and all your kinfolks are proud to say they know a successful author.

Then you get a letter from your editor, suggesting that your stories aren't quite racy enough for the market. You need to add characters and scenes that you find offensive.

If writing is all you know how to do, you'll compromise and find ways of justifying it. "We have to pay the mortgage. Our daughter is going to college in the fall." You'll start writing books you're not proud of. Maybe you'll write them under another name, but when you're alone with yourself, you won't be proud.

I've known writers who were ashamed of what they wrote. At writing conventions, they would gather in a bar and talk late into the night about how "we're all hacks."

You're a hack if you allow yourself to be a hack. It's a choice.

I always felt that I could find a way of making an honest living: punch cows, drive a bulldozer, sell real estate, work as a handyman. And I've never published a book that would have shamed my mother.

20. Don't write anything that would shame your mother.

It sounds terribly old-fashioned, but I think it's good advice. Isaac Botkin offered the same advice to young filmmakers and needed only five words to say it: "Seek virtue and study nobility." [Botkin 2006:198]

Bibliography

Botkin, Isaac. *Outside Hollywood,* Vision Forum Ministries, 2007.

Davies, Paul. *God and the New Physics.* Simon and Schuster, 1983.

Davies, Paul. *The Mind of God: The Scientific Basis For a Rational World.* Simon and Schuster, 1992.

Farris, Michael. *From Tyndale to Madison: How the Death of an English Martyr Led to the American Bill of Rights.* B & H Publishing Group, 2007.

Feynman, Richard. *The Character of Physical Law.* MIT Press, 1965.

Feynman, Richard. *The Pleasure of Finding Things Out.* Perseus Publishing, 1999.

Foster-Harris. *The Basic Formulas of Fiction.* University of Oklahoma Press, 1967.

Glaspey, Terry. *Not a Tame Lion: The Spiritual Legacy of C.S. Lewis and the Chronicles of Narnia.* Cumberland House 2005.

Kavanaugh, Patrick. *The Spiritual Lives of the Great Composers.* Sparrow Press, 1992.

King James Bible. The World Publishing Company, 1953.

Kugel, James L. *How To Read The Bible: A Guide To Scripture, Then and Now.* Free Press, 2007.

Lewerenz, Spencer and Barbara Nicolosi. Thom Parham, "Why Do Heathens Make the Best Christian Films?" And Linda Seger, "What Kind of Stories Should We Tell?" *Behind the Screen: Hollywood Insiders on Faith, Film and Culture.* Baker Books, 2005.

Lewis, C.S. *Christian Reflections.* Wm. B. Eerdmans Publishing Co., 1995.

Lewis, C.S. *The Complete C.S. Lewis Signature Classics.* HarperCollins, 2002.

Lewis, C.S. *Mere Christianity.* Harper Collins, 2001.

Lewis, C.S. *The Seeing Eye and Other Selected Essays From Christian Reflections.* Ballantine Books, 1967.

Living Bible Paraphrased. Tyndale House Publishers, 1971.

McGrath, Charles. "Norman Mailer, Towering Writer with a Matching Ego, Dies at 84." *New York Times,* November 11, 2007.

The New International Version Study Bible. Zondervan Publishing House, 1973.

Olasky, Marvin. "Goodnight, Hoppers; Goodnight, Hustlers Everywhere." *World Magazine.* July 26, 2008.

Olasky, Susan. "Interview with John R. Erickson." *World Magazine,* December 2, 2006.

Pearcey, Nancy. *Total Truth,* Crossway Books, 2004.

Pearcey, Nancy, Harold Fickett, Charles Colson. *How Now Shall We Live?* Tyndale House Publishers, Inc., 1999.

Penrose, Roger. *The Emperor's New Mind: Concerning Computers, Minds, and the Laws of Physics.* Penguin Books, 1989.

Ryken, Philip Graham. *Art For God's Sake: A Call to Recover the Arts.* P & R Publishing Co., 2006.

Schaeffer, Francis A. *Art and the Bible.* InterVarsity Press, 1973.

Schaeffer, Francis A. *Genesis in Space and Time,* 1972.

Schaeffer, Francis A. *The Complete Works of Francis A. Schaeffer,* Volume 1. Crossway Books, 1985.

Schaeffer, Francis A. *The Complete Works of Francis A. Schaeffer,* Volume 5. Crossway Books, 1985.

Schaeffer, Francis A. *How Should We Then Live?* Crossway Books, 1976.

Tame, David. *The Secret Power of Music.* Destiny Books, 1984.

Veith, Gene Edward, Jr. *God At Work: Your Christian Vocation in All of Life.* Crossway Books Focal Point Series, 2002.

Veith, Gene Edward, Jr. *Postmodern Times: A Christian Guide to Contemporary Thought and Culture.* Crossway Books, 1994.

Veith, Gene Edward, Jr. *Reading Between the Lines: A Christian Guide To Literature.* Crossway Books, 1990.

Veith, Gene Edward, Jr. *The Soul of Prince Caspian: Exploring Spiritual Truth in the Land of Narnia.* David C. Cook, 2008.

Veith, Gene Edward Jr. *State of the Arts: From Bezalel to Mapplethorpe.* Crossway Books, 1991.

INFORMATION ABOUT THE PUBLISHERS

MAVERICK BOOKS:

In 1982, John and Kris Erickson started Maverick Books in their garage in Perryton, Texas. John had spent fifteen years collecting rejection slips from publishers and either had to give up or do something different. He chose the latter and has never looked back. Hank the Cowdog became the star of a popular series of family/children's books, and eventually found a home with a major national publisher, Viking/Penguin. Maverick Books remains the publisher of the audio books and also sells Hank books and merchandise through www.hankthecowdog.com.

PATRICK HENRY COLLEGE:

At Patrick Henry College, students receive a broad-based baccalaureate education that stresses content, the imitation of excellence, the pursuit of knowledge, and the exercise of the whole range of talents that God has given, in the light of the truth that He has revealed in the inerrant Bible. The 75-credit core curriculum—consisting of courses in logic, rhetoric, philosophy, mathematics, geometry, music, science, history, literature, theology, apologetics, economics, foreign languages, constitutional law, and political theory--lays a common foundation for advanced learning in each of five major programs. Within the context of the classical liberal arts as a time-tested framework, courses mirror the trivium's emphasis on knowledge (grammar), understanding (logic), and application (rhetoric). The culmination of a PHC student's education is an apprenticeship in which to apply the "rhetoric" of creative performance in the field of study. Regardless of major, students are invited to explore the interconnectedness of all the disciplines reflecting the truth that in Christ "all things hold together" (Colossians 1:17).

INDEX

A

Abbott, Jack Henry, 80
ACLU, 90
Adverbs, 70, 135
Aesthetic, 4, 69, 78, 109, 115, 118-120
African Queen, The, 114
Africans, 120
Alaska (Fairbanks), 24
Amarillo Symphony, 67
America, 16, 20, 34, 42, 79, 89-90
American Cowboy, 129
American Gothic, 92
American, xvii, 3, 28, 34, 52, 60, 71, 80-81, 92, 94, 106, 125, 129, 152
Amis, Martin, 80
Amish, 42
Anatevka, 74
Aramaic, 120
Archeology, 10
Arctic, 141
Arizona, 32, 94
Arizona, Chinle, 94
Arizona, Winslow, 94
Asians, 120
Atlantic Monthly, 126
Audio Book, 23, 25, 28, 53, 163,
Australian Shepherd Dog, 14
Author, x, xiv, xv, xvi, xviii, xx, 1-3, 8-9, 18, 20, 22-23, 27, 34-35, 43-46, 48, 51, 53, 55-56, 63, 77, 79, 83, 89, 96, 101, 107, 112-113, 117, 120, 126, 128-129, 133, 135, 145, 151, 153-156
Author's Liability, 77
Autism, 104-105
Azusa Pacific University, 110

B

Babe, 85
Babylonians, 76
Bambi, 44
Baptist, 26, 62, 67, 121
Basic Formulas of Fiction, The, 70
Beauty, xi, 58, 63, 67, 69, 70, 72-75, 77, 82,
103, 106, 118-121, 126
Because of Winn-Dixie, 86
Beery, Wallace, 114
Bergson, 132
Best Seller, 126
Bible, 7, 10, 54, 57, 63, 65-66, 92, 95, 135, 153
Biblical Characters, 7 (Joseph), 7, 8 (David), 4,5 (Paul), 7 (Samuel), 7 (Sampson), 5 (Ramses), 5,7,8 (Moses)
Big Media, xvi, xviii
Black, Baxter, 141
Bohm, David, 73, 119
Bohm, L. Frank, 93,
Bombeck, Erma, 142
Book, John, 42
Botkin, Isaac, 29, 35, 111, 157
Bricklayer, 129-130,
Brooks, Garth, 9
Brothers Karamazov, The, 117
Buena Vista Drive, 39
Bugs Bunny, xi, 85
Burbank, 39

C

California, 36, 38, 43, 141
Canadian River, 128-129
Captain Kangaroo, 31
Carpenter, 75, 129
Cartoon, xii, xviii, 27, 31, 33, 66, 85
Cartoonist, 25, 46
Casablanca, 114
Case of the Blazing Sky, The, 102
Case of the Midnight Rustler, The, 53
Case of the Tricky Trap, The, 100-101
Casso, Carlos, 53
Catholic, 62, 65, 67
Cattleman Magazine, The, 14-15, 21, 128, 147
CBS, xii, xviii, 27, 31-32, 34, 36, 65, 68
Chaplin, Charlie, 78
Chaucer, xiii
Chemistry, 56-59, 152

Cherokee, 94
Chesterton, xiii
Chicago, 12
Chicken, x, xvi, 21, 32, 99-102
Chinese, 28, 62, 121
Christian Art, 109, 113, 120-121
Christian Artist, xiii
Christian Law of Gravity, 120
Christian, x, xi, xiii, xiv, xvii, xviii, 1, 3, 29, 30, 42, 48, 54, 57-58, 60, 61, 62, 66, 69, 76, 81-82, 88-93, 95, 96-97, 102-103, 109-115, 117-121, 126, 139, 148, 155
Christianity, xv, xiii, xvii, xviii, 60, 132
Chronicles of Narnia, The, xviii, 96
Church, xi, xii, xvii, 2, 4, 12, 24, 34, 54, 56, 60, 65-67, 72, 110, 117, 121, 142
Cinderella, 40
Classical, xiv, 54, 60, 163
Clay, George, xx
Cold Weather Cowdog Blues, The, 24
Comanche, 144
Comedy, x, xiii, 74, 77-78, 86, 97
Composting, 55
Confessions of a Cowdog, 15, 128
Constantine, 60
Constitution, U.S., 81
Cooper, Jackie, 114
Cowboy, x, xvi, xix, 2, 7, 13-15, 20-22, 32, 51, 53, 57, 94, 101, 126, 128-129, 141, 148
Craft, xii, xiii, xiv, xix, 3-4, 16, 29, 57-58, 69, 76, 79, 81, 88, 111, 114, 130-131
Craftsman, 181
Craftsmanship, 76
Creative, xii, xvi, 4, 27, 51, 55-56, 63, 82, 106, 147, 151
Cross, 113
Cross, Frank Moore, 10
Crucifixion, 109
Curse of the Incredible Priceless Corncob, The, 99
Czarist, 141

D

Dahlstrom, Nathan, xx
Damascus, 110
Dante, xiii, 20, 116, 120
Darwin, 66
Davies, Paul, 72-73
Dayton, Todd, 23

Dead Sea Scrolls, 10
Decalogue, 76
Democrat, 62
DePauw University, 24
Devil in Texas and Other Cowboy Tales, The, 15, 21
Diagram, 70-71, 133-134
Dialog, 56
Dickens, 1, 13, 120
Didactic, 96
Dirac, Paul, 73, 119
Disciples of Christ, 67
Disney (Studios), xii, 35-41, 43-48, 85, 155
Disney, Roy Jr., 40, 46
Disney, Walt, 36-38, 40, 44-46, 48, 85
Divine Intelligence, 97-98
Domestic, 58
Dostoyevsky, 20, 141
Doyle, Sir Author Conan, 141
Dream Machine (also, "Dream Factory"), 38-39
Drover, xi, xv, 15, 32, 77, 101, 128
Dumas, 13
Dykema, Kristine, 9
Dyslexic, 104, 108

E

East Coast, 35
Eastern Publishers, 16
Ecclesiastes, 135
Eden, 42
Egyptian, 92, 120
Einstein, 73, 119
Ellis Theatre, 41
English, 6, 45, 65-66, 94, 106, 121, 133, 142,
Enkidu, 69
Epic of Gilgamesh, The, 69, 120
Episodic, 36-38
Erickson, Anna Beth Curry, 7; Ashley, 32; John, x, xii, xiv-xvi, xviii-xix, xxi, , 7-8,18, 40, 89, 93, 128; Kris, xiv, xx-xxi, 10-12, 20, 22-23, 25, 35-37, 39, 57, 66, 126, 147, 163; Mark, xx, 22, 25, 32, 95; Scot, 26, 32
E.T., 86
Ethical, 4, 83, 109,
Ethics, 34, 66, 83,
European, 125
Europeans, Southern, 120
Eye-Crosserosis, 93

167

Southern, xvii, 62, 120
Soviet Gulag, 141
Spiritual, 4, 56, 58, 60, 63, 81, 102-103, 105,
   106, 108-109, 121, 153
St. Augustine, 120
Stendhal, Krister, 10
Stephen, 110
Story Structure, 69-70, 74, 76, 78, 83, 109, 150
Storycraft, xix, 88, 111
Storyteller, xix, 7, 61, 71, 76, 109, 111-113, 125
Storytelling, xii-xiii, 8, 14, 63, 69, 70, 76-77,
   96-97, 105, 109, 111, 116
Strindberg, 52
Strong's Concordance of the Bible, 92
Strugnell, John, 10
Sunday School, xi
Swift, xiii

T

Tevis, Trev, 24
Tango, 148
Ten Commandments, 76, 81, 147
Testament, New, 61, 92
Testament, Old, 10, 112, 117
Tevye, 74-75
Texana, 16
Texas Home School Coalition, xxi, 107
Texas Monthly, 25
Texas Monthly Press, 27
Texas, 1, 9, 11-12, 15, 35, 41, 43, 46, 52, 62,
   89, 149; Amarillo, 23, 37, 38, 67; Austin, 12,
   27, 35, 39, 140; Dallas, 9, 43; Fort Worth,
   35; Glen Rose, 129; Houston, 27, 10;
   Hutchinson County, 128; Lubbock, xix, 7;
   Panhandle, 14, 32, 51, 107, 128, 148; Perryton, 6,
   12, 14, 20-21, 24-26, 31, 38, 66, 128, 162
Texas, Roberts County, xxi,
Texas, West, xvii, 5, 20, 57, 65, 141, 148
The THSC Review, xxi
Thomas, Norman, 10
Thorn Birds, The, 112
Tillich, 132
Time's Square, 121
Tolstoy, 13, 120
Tom and Jerry, 85
Tom Sawyer, xvii
Torah, 75
Total Truth, xv, 1, 139
Tradecraft, 79

Tragedy, xiii, 42, 74, 107, 116
Trajectory, 77
Treasure Island, 114, 115
Twain, Mark, xvii, 1, 13, 141
Tyndale, William, 65-66

U

Union Theological Seminary, 10
United States, 22, 25, 56, 126, 154
Univerity of Texas, 6, 10, 139
University of North Texas Press, 13
University of Oklahoma, 70
Updike, John, 11
Uppercase Art, 79, 81-82
Uppercase Artist, 119
Utah, 80

V

Veith, Gene Edward, x, xx, 2-3, 51, 54, 60, 67, 69,
   74, 95-96, 104, 111, 116, 118, 120, 125, 151
Vidal, 13
Viking-Penguin, 27
Viola, 94
Virgil, 116
Virginia, 29
Vocation, xi-xiv, xx, 2, 8, 51, 54, 56-58, 81,
   125, 146,

W

Waugh, Evelyn, xiii
Wayland Baptist University, 26
West Coast, 39
Western Civilization, xiv, 10, 60, 80, 82
Western Hemisphere, 46
Western Horseman, 14
Western Society, xviii
Wisdom, xxi, 7, 54, 63, 69, 72, 76, 85, 88, 90, 142
Witness, 41-43
Womanhood, 58
Wood, Grant, 92
Woody Woodpecker, 85
World Magazine, 94, 101
World War II, 6, 115, 135, 141
Worldview, xvii-xviii, 3, 4, 34, 42, 48, 58, 60,
   61, 63, 65-66, 95, 97, 103, 118-119, 139
Wouk, Herman, 141
Wright, G. Earnest, 10
Writer's Block, 151-152,
Writer's Market, 155